Undergraduate Topics in Computer Science

'Undergraduate Topics in Computer Science' (UTiCS) delivers high-quality instructional content for undergraduates studying in all areas of computing and information science. From core foundational and theoretical material to final-year topics and applications, UTiCS books take a fresh, concise, and modern approach and are ideal for self-study or for a one- or two-semester course. The texts are all authored by established experts in their fields, reviewed by an international advisory board, and contain numerous examples and problems, many of which include fully worked solutions.

The UTiCS concept relies on high-quality, concise books in softback format, and generally a maximum of 275-300 pages. For undergraduate textbooks that are likely to be longer, more expository, Springer continues to offer the highly regarded Texts in Computer Science series, to which we refer potential authors.

More information about this series at http://www.springer.com/series/7592

Kingsley Sage

Concise Guide to Object-Oriented Programming

An Accessible Approach Using Java

 Springer

Kingsley Sage
School of Engineering and Informatics
University of Sussex
Falmer, East Sussex, UK

ISSN 1863-7310   ISSN 2197-1781   (electronic)
Undergraduate Topics in Computer Science
ISBN 978-3-030-13303-0   ISBN 978-3-030-13304-7   (eBook)
https://doi.org/10.1007/978-3-030-13304-7

Library of Congress Control Number: 2019931822

This Springer imprint is published by the registered company Springer Nature Switzerland AG
The registered company address is: Gewerbestrasse 11, 6330 Cham, Switzerland

Preface

The twenty-first century continues to experience the relentless expansion of the IT revolution into our daily lives. We consume services, do our shopping on-line, listen to music streams and watch movies on demand. The impact of social media has had a profound impact on our society and has changed fundamentally the way we obtain and consume news, information and ideas. There is little sign of a slowdown in this dramatic shift in our relationship with technology. Vast research budgets are being applied to the development of autonomous vehicles, and in applying Artificial Intelligence to change the way we live. But it has also changed the demand for skills within our workforce. The demand for manual skills is in decline, and the demand for IT and programming skills is rising at an unprecedented rate.

In comparison to the industrialists of the nineteenth and twentieth centuries, the twenty-first-century entrepreneurs are experts in IT, programming, software design and development, and developing practical applications using concepts such as Artificial Intelligence for our daily lives. With this profound paradigm shift has come a need for the workforce of many industrialised nations to evolve. Governments recognise the need for a huge increase in the workforce with programming skills. In the United Kingdom, and in many other industrialised nations, core coding skills are now a part of the secondary school curriculum. Learning to program is no longer considered to be just a part of the traditional journey of the Computer Science undergraduate, but a broader skill that underpins an IT literate workforce for the modern age.

What is the Purpose of This Book?

When I was first approached to write this book, it was suggested that its purpose was to provide an accessible introduction to coding and the world of Object Oriented Programming (OOP). Standard texts on the subject often fall between those that provide only a very lightweight treatment of the subject ("a little knowledge can be a frustrating thing"), and those that run to 500 pages or more that are rather better suited as reference texts or as support on a lengthy period of study in depth. The challenge for this book is to provide an accessible introduction to the world of coding and OOP in a way that is helpful to the first-time coder and allows them to develop and to understand their knowledge and skills in a way that is relevant and practical. The examples developed for this book are intended to show how OOP skills can be used to create applications and programs that have everyday value, rather than examples that have been synthesised solely to demonstrate an academic point.

The reader should be able to use this book to develop a solid appreciation of OOP and how to code. The programming language used throughout is Java. Java has been chosen as it can be used across all computing platforms, because it has a commercial skill that has a clear on-going value derived from its adoption as a core language for smartphone applications on the Android platform, and as the language at the heart of the Java EE 8 Jakarta Enterprise scale framework. The book focusses on the core Java language and does not consider smartphone or EE 8 coding, as these require skills over and above what this book is about. However, a knowledge of core Java coding and some of the related issues also discussed in this book would form an appropriate pre-requisite for the further study of these topics.

Although this book uses Java as its illustrative programming language, many of the ideas may be translated directly into other OO languages such as C++, C# and others. Throughout this book, programming in Java is demonstrated using the BlueJ Integrated Development Environment (IDE). BlueJ is a well-established IDE for learning BlueJ and is widely used in schools and Universities. Eclipse is the closest product to an industry standard for the development of Java, but it is often found too complex for the task of teaching and learning.

Who is This Book Aimed at?

As someone with over 20 years of teaching experience from level 3 through to postgraduate, from traditional University teaching to adult education, I have never been able to identify satisfactorily what defines the ability of an individual to learn to program. Suffice to say, all that is really needed is an interest in the subject and time. The aim of this book is to provide an accessible entry into the world of Object Oriented Programming (OOP).

The book does not assume any prior knowledge of coding, or any prior knowledge of software engineering or OO, not does it require any prior exposure to mathematics. Whilst such prior knowledge is not unhelpful, it is not essential to learn to program. Instead, this book takes a more everyday experience to the subject, drawing on examples from everyday experience to explain what OO is and why it is relevant in the modern programming experience. As such, the book is aimed at those who are coming to OO programming for the first time. It is therefore likely to be useful as a one-semester book introducing the topic to those new to the study of computer science at the undergraduate and postgraduate levels, and those who are just learning for the purpose of self-improvement or professional development. Whilst the book is aimed at those with no prior coding experience, it does explore broader topics surrounding coding. This with some prior knowledge may opt to skip some of the early chapters. That does not impact the usefulness of this book in terms of learning to code in Java.

What's in the Book?

Chapter 1 starts with an overview of what programming and coding is all about. It includes some useful historical perspective on the development of programming languages and the core ideas that underpin all programming languages. It introduces the idea of a computing machine and concepts such as a compiler. This section is helpful to those who have no prior experience of computing as it helps subsequent understanding of some of the core coding processes and terminology. The chapter then continues to discuss how the need for OOP arose in the period from the end of the 1970s to the present day, and a discussion of why it is considered important to help us solve modern-day programming problems.

Chapter 2 provides a short introduction to programming in Java using BlueJ. It is intended to provide just enough knowledge and skills to create and execute a single-class Java program under BlueJ. This is significant as it then facilitates discussion of the core principles of procedural and structured programming, such as loops and conditional statements. Those with prior experience of coding using languages such as C and Python may opt to skip this chapter, as they would undoubtedly be familiar with much of the content. I chose to organise the book this way as the basic procedural and structured coding constructions are common to almost all programming (or at least those that owe their syntactic ancestry to C), and getting these constructions understood at this stage allows for a more specific focus later on the principles of OO.

Chapter 3 gets into the details of what OO really is and how it can be applied to solve modern programming challenges. We start with a discussion of what classes and objects are, and how the construction and execution of an OO program parallels the way that human organisations such as a large office operate. Such analogies are invaluable in appreciating the true benefits of the OO paradigm. In this chapter, we develop a set of small multi-class Java applications and consider the cornerstone issues in OO design of class cohesion and coupling.

Chapter 4 considers a range of Java library objects and packages such as the `String` and the `ArrayList`, and introduces the idea of the Application Programming Interface (API). This enables the reader to start building more complex applications involving simple linear collections of objects. These ideas are developed using a set of simple programs that can be enhanced in many different ways as an exercise for the reader.

Chapter 5 delves further into the OO paradigm and considers how OO design forms an essential part of producing a useful solution to a problem. The chapter introduces the idea of class polymorphism (super and sub-classes) and how this can be used to create a program with a structure that more closely mirrors an underlying domain. The chapter also looks further into the idea of selecting classes that are suited to solving specific problem and so also has elements of software engineering principles and practice.

Chapter 6 considers what to do when code encounters an error condition. Software systems are not immune to errors either at the coding or at the run time phases, and modern software systems need to be built in a robust manner so that they behave in a predictable manner when something goes wrong. The exception handling mechanism is introduced, along with steps on laying out a program to assist in debugging it. This chapter also considers practical measures that are adopted in defensive coding.

Chapter 7 digs deeper into the work of arrays and collections, notably fixed length arrays, the HashMap and HashSet, and shows how different collection types can be used to effectively model different real-world collections of data. This chapter also includes some background on the underlying ideas for these collection types, such as the hash table.

Chapter 8 provides an introduction to building a Graphical User Interface (GUI) using Swing. Although some may consider Swing a relatively old library for the development of a GUI, the key ideas are relevant across a range of other libraries such as JavaFX, and Swing forms more of a core element of the Java landscape. The development of GUIs is a large topic in its own right, so this chapter can only ever serve as an introduction. In this chapter, we also consider the concept of a design pattern, specifically the idea of Model View Controller (MVC) architecture, and how a Java application can be constructed in a well-recognisable design configuration.

In the final Chap. 9, two complete applications are presented, from conceptual design to implementation to help cement the ideas presented in the previous chapters. One is a text-based application with no Graphical User Interface (GUI). The other is a small GUI-based application to give a sense of how to build a GUI on top of an underlying application.

All the code examples used in this book and the two example projects described in Chap. 9 are available as on-line resource accompanying this book.

It is my hope that this book will inspire the reader to learn more about the world of OO and coding. As such, it represents the start of a learning journey. As with all endeavours, clarity will improve with time and effort. Few will write an award-winning book at their first attempt. Few artists will paint their defining masterpiece at the outset of their career. Programming is no exception and your skills will improve with effort, time, reflection and experience. But every learning journey has to start somewhere. For many, the story starts with the codebreakers of Bletchley Park in the United Kingdom during WWII, but we shall start our story in early nineteenth-century France …

Falmer, UK   Kingsley Sage
January 2019

Contents

1 The Origins of Programming 1
   1.1   The Stored Digital Program is not a New Idea 1
   1.2   The Birth of the Computing Age 3
   1.3   The Origin of Programming Languages 4
   1.4   The Object Oriented Revolution 6
   1.5   The Java Language 7
   1.6   Tools of the Trade 8

2 Procedural Programming Basics in Java 11
   2.1   First Program and Workflow 11
   2.2   Primitive Data Types 16
   2.3   The Procedural Programming Paradigm 19
   2.4   Sequence 20
   2.5   Alternation 22
   2.6   Repetition 25
   2.7   More on Methods 29
   2.8   Bringing It All Together 32

3 Getting into Object Oriented Programming 37
   3.1   Object Oriented in a Social Context 37
   3.2   Introducing the OO Class 39
   3.3   The Anatomy of a Class 40
   3.4   Creating Objects at Run Time 47
   3.5   Accessor and Mutator Methods 52
   3.6   Choosing the Right Classes 55

4 Library Classes and Packages 57
   4.1   Organisation of Java into the Core and Packages 57
   4.2   Using Library Classes 58
   4.3   The String Class 59
   4.4   Application Programming Interfaces (APIs) 62
   4.5   Using Javadocs in BlueJ 64

4.6   The `ArrayList` Class   67
4.7   The Wrapper Classes   72

5   Modelling the World the Object Oriented Way   75
5.1   Hierarchies in the Real World   75
5.2   Introducing Super and Sub-classes   77
5.3   Adding Constructors   81
5.4   Rules of Inheritance and Over-Riding   82
5.5   Method Polymorphism   86
5.6   Static and Dynamic Type   88
5.7   Abstract Classes   90
5.8   Interfaces   92
5.9   Class Variables and Static Methods   95

6   Dealing with Errors   99
6.1   The Nature of Errors   99
6.2   Coding Defensively 101
6.3   Using the Debugger Tool 104
6.4   Unit Testing 108
6.5   System Testing 115
6.6   The Basics of Exception Handling 116
6.7   More Advanced Exception Handling 121

7   Deeper into Arrays and Collections 123
7.1   Fixed Length Versus Dynamic Length Arrays 123
7.2   Fixed Length Arrays of Primitive Types 124
7.3   Fixed Length Arrays of Objects 126
7.4   Multi-dimensional Arrays 127
7.5   Sorting Data 130
7.6   Hash Functions 136
7.7   The `HashMap` Class 138
7.8   The `HashSet` Class 141
7.9   Iterating Through Collections 143

8   Adding a Graphical User Interface 147
8.1   The Model View Controller MVC Design Pattern 148
8.2   Introducing Swing and AWT 151
8.3   The Taxonomy of a GUI 152
8.4   A Simple First Swing Application 153
8.5   Event Handling 156
8.6   Centralised and Distributed Event Management 158
8.7   Applying the MVC Design Pattern 162
8.8   Adding Menus, Text Fields, Text Areas and Images 167
8.9   Layout Managers 172

9 Example Applications 179
  9.1 Software Engineering Process Models 179
  9.2 The Good Life Foods Project 180
  9.3 The Guessing Game Project 186
  9.4 Final Thoughts 189

Index 191

About the Author

Dr. Kingsley Sage is a Senior Teaching Fellow in Computing Sciences in the Department of Informatics at the University of Sussex, Brighton, UK, and a Senior Fellow of the Higher Education Academy (SFHEA). He has more than 20 years of teaching experience, from the level of further/continuing education through to postgraduate-level teaching, in both traditional university teaching and adult education.

The Origins of Programming

1

In this first chapter we explore what a programming language is, and something of the history of their development leading up to the Java language. This will help us understand some of the most basic terminology used in the process of creating programs. The history of programming, and computing in general, does not have a universally agreed timeline and shared sense of significance of contributions. Nonetheless, computer science has progressed and innovated to bring us a world that we may scarcely consider without its plurality of systems with software, data and programs at their core.

1.1 The Stored Digital Program is not a New Idea

Whereas the digital electronic computer is a 20th century concept, the idea of digital control goes back much further. Digital control simply refers to the idea of a system controlled by a sequence of instructions that are either 1 or 0, "on" or "off". One of earliest notable examples of such a system that used stored digital instructions was the Jacquard weaving loom. In the early 1800s, Joseph-Marie Jacquard (1752–1834) developed an automated weaving loom using a series of punched paper cards to control the head of the loom to raise and lower different threads to permit a wide range of fabric designs to be mass produced. Any design could be expressed by the set of punched cards that were fed to the machine.

© Springer Nature Switzerland AG 2019
K. Sage, *Concise Guide to Object-Oriented Programming*,
Undergraduate Topics in Computer Science,
https://doi.org/10.1007/978-3-030-13304-7_1

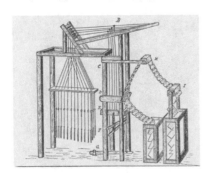 

Sources https://commons.wikimedia.org/wiki/File:Book_Illustration,_Jacquard_Weaving_and_Designing,_
Falcon_Loom_of_1728,_Figure_12,_1895_(CH_68766143).jpg (public domain) https://commons.wikim
edia.org/wiki/File:Jacquard.loom.cards.jpg (public domain)

Jacquard's ideas were a step innovation of previous work by Jacques de Vaucanson (1709–1782) and others, but Jacquard is usually credited with creating a
commercial scale automated weaving loom that made use of stored digital data.
This idea proved inspirational for others in the development of computer science.
For example, Charles Babbage used punched cards as a means of input and output
for his designs for the analytical engine—an early calculating device. As all data,
whether numeric, text, image or audio, can be formulated into an equivalent binary
representation, such cards provided a convenient means of storing data. For
example, the number 19 in denary (base 10) can be converted into binary (base 2).

2^4	2^3	2^2	2^1	2^0
16	8	4	2	1
1	0	0	1	1

Here 19 = 1 + 2 + 16. Individual letters can be assigned to numeric values (i.e.
the ASCII code set) and thus text can be converted into a sequence of numbers, and
thus binary data. Continuous data can be "sampled" at regular intervals and those
samples can be converted to numbers and subsequently to binary data.

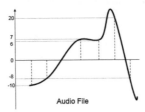

1.2 The Birth of the Computing Age

Pioneers such as Charles Babbage (1791–1871) strove to create mechanical calculating devices such as the Difference Engine (1830s) and the rather more general purpose Analytical Engine (unfinished in Babbage's lifetime). The latter is recognisable by design in many respects as a computer, as it featured a set of instructions stored on punched cards, a memory that could remember results, and elements of sequential control. However, Babbage was ahead of his time in that the engineering challenges posed in building his mechanical machines were substantial. But many of his ideas laid dormant until new forms of technology emerged from the new sciences of electricity and electronics.

In 1936, the British mathematician Alan Turing (1912–1954) published his seminal paper "On Computable Numbers". In it, he describes an abstract computing apparatus called a "Turing machine"—a type of universal machine that Turing was able to demonstrate, using mathematics, could compute all computable things.

Source https://en.wikipedia.org/wiki/Alan_Turing (public domain)

The machine consisted of a paper tape of infinite length that enabled read and write operations to be performed. Depending on the symbol observed on the tape, the tape can be made to move forwards and backwards. Turing is actually describing the underlying requirements of a modern computer and a programming language—a feat given that in 1936 the technologies needed to realise such devices barely existed.

Turing and others would later realise electronic implementations of Turing machines using electronic valve and later transistor technology, allowing the realisation of general purpose "electronic digital computers". Turing is also widely credited for popularising the term "Artificial Intelligence" as he believed that one day such digital computers would rival humans for computing and analytical ability.

The onset of World War 2 brought opportunities for Turing and others in the form of the Allied effort to decipher Nazi Germany's secretive Enigma codes, particularly in respect of minimising shipping losses to U-boats on the North Atlantic supply route (the "Battle of the Atlantic"). U-boat command used Enigma machines, a type of modified electronic typewriter, to convert plain text messages to cipher text that was then broadcast by radio to the U-boats. Recovering the original plain text required another Enigma machine with identical settings to the original. The design was such that there were billions of combinations of settings and it was statistically unlikely they could be discovered by chance. A group of scientists, including Turing, worked at the Bletchley Park site in England to build a range of machines, such as Turing's Bombe and later the Colossus device, that could sift through millions of settings in just a few hours to find the correct one.

Source   https://en.wikipedia.org/wiki/File:Wartime_picture_of_a_Bletchley_Park_Bombe.jpg   (public domain) https://en.wikipedia.org/wiki/Colossus_computer (public domain)

This was the start of the era of cryptoanalysis. Colossus is regarded by many as the world's first semi programmable electronic computer, and a faithful recreation of the machine can be viewed today at the UK's National Machine of Computing at Bletchley Park.

The post-war years were less kind on Turing, with events leading to his suicide in 1954. But the development of electronic computers continued apace in the UK and the US, with the development of machines such as the Manchester Mk 1 (UK, 1949) and ENIAC (US, 1945). 1952 heralded the arrival of the Ferranti Mk 1, the world's first commercially available general-purpose computer.

1.3   The Origin of Programming Languages

By the 1950s, computer hardware was a reality. But as with all technologies, the question arose of what it should be used for. ENIAC was initially developed to produce artillery firing tables for the US army—a repetitive and time-consuming task suited to a machine. The Manchester Mark 1 was used for tasks including searching for prime numbers and investigating the Riemann hypothesis.

The issue was the relatively low amounts of computing power combined with the fact that there was only a small group of experts who truly understood how to program the machines. Initially machines were programmed using binary and very near binary "assembly languages" supported by mnemonic aids. Creating programs at such a low level required a great deal of time and intellect.

The idea of a higher-level view of a computing problem is widely credited to Ada Lovelace (1815–1852), who collaborated with Charles Babbage and wrote notes on the design of algorithms for Babbage's machines. Whilst not programs, these algorithms represented a higher-level way of thinking about what a computing device could do.

The key development was to provide a means for programs to be written in a higher level, more human centric manner, that could then be translated into the lower level binary instructions that a computer could process. The earliest programming languages included "Short Code" (John Mauchly 1950) and "Autocode" (Alick Glennie and Ralph Brooker 1954). These languages allowed a source code file to be created with the high-level instructions, that were then "compiled" or "interpreted" into the lower level instructions that the computer could execute:

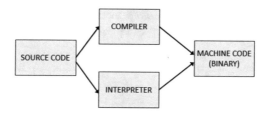

Compiled languages made the translation one-time and then stored the resulting machine code for execution many times over. Interpreted languages made the translation "on the fly" for immediate use. This distinction is still very much in evidence today, with languages such as C and Java belonging to the compiled group, and scripting languages such as JavaScript and PHP belonging to the interpreted group. The interpreted group has become particularly significant in the world of web computing.

1954 saw the development of FORTRAN by a team lead by John Backus at IBM. This was a very significant innovation as FORTRAN was the first widely adopted general purpose programming language and it still exists today, although it has long since fallen from wide use. Other notable languages include COBOL (for business related programming tasks) (Grace Hopper, 1959) and LISP (for symbolic computing) (Russell, Hart and Levin, 1958). Nearly all these early languages are now a matter of historical note, but 1972 brought a significant milestone with the arrival of C (Bell Labs, Dennis Ritchie). C was significant as it brought a consistent syntax, provided a range of high and low level instructions and operations, was designed to encourage cross platform support, was (and still is) the subject of international standardisation. C was used to write the UNIX 4 operating system (still very much in use today). C is also significant in that many contemporary programming languages (including Java) owe their syntactic history to it. C has also seen a reboot in the form of the object oriented C++. Now a wide range of people could write programs using high-level abstraction rather than needing to understand the detailed internal operation of the host computer.

1.4   The Object Oriented Revolution

As computers became cheaper, more widespread and powerful, the range of applications that they were put to increased. In the 1950s, computers were mainly used for mathematical and scientific tasks, by the 1970s they were in wide use in business data management, and with the explosion of personal computing in the 1980s, they reached out into every aspect of modern lives. That expansion of ambition for creating ever new and more innovative program applications came with its own challenges—the size and complexity of codebases was increasing:

Typical codebase size	
1950s	10s of lines
1960s	100s of lines
1970s	1000s of lines
1980s	100,000s of code
Now	In some cases > 10,000,000 lines (e.g. Linux)

The challenge here is not technological, it's human. By the 1970s, a significant number of software development projects were failing (i.e. required substantial or complete write-down of their costs due to failure to deliver a working product) as they were becoming too complex for teams to develop and manage using the programming languages and techniques available. This period saw the birth of software engineering as an academic discipline to try to counter this. The problem lay in the fact that they kind of data employed by programming languages was based in mathematical and fundamental terms like characters, integers and pointers. These are not the atomic elements that were needed to build something like a graphic computer game, or a word processor. Humans don't think of most problem domains in atomic terms. We think of them in terms of entities like "Player", "Paragraph" and a "Spell checker" and so on.

So there was a basic mismatch between the programming concepts on offer and the problem domains that developers wanted to address. Furthermore, a program written for one computer would not necessarily execute on another. By the 1980s there was a proliferation of competing brands of computer, with little or no inter-operability between them.

In 1967, the Simula language (Dahl, Nygaard) was the first Object Oriented (OO) language. In 1980, Smalltalk-80 (Kay, Ingalls and Goldberg) was released, drawing heavily on Simula for inspiration. These languages were developed part in response to the challenges faced by ever expanding code base sizes and part by the need to express solutions in a human centric manner. Smalltalk is significant in the programming language development timeline as it directly influenced the design of a generation of OO languages such C++, Flavors and Java. Smalltalk had at its centre the concept of a "class" as an organisational unit of a program, capable of describing a meaningful entity that formed part of the problem domain. Instances of these classes ("objects") could then message each other to work together to solve some collective problem, much as a team of people would communicate and cooperate to solve a problem. The world has never looked back, and the OO paradigm is now an established cornerstone of our modern programming landscape.

1.5   The Java Language

The Java language had its 1990s origins in a language called Oak intended for use in interactive television set top boxes. Initially developed by James Gosling, Michael Sheridan and Patrick Naughton, the aim was to produce an OO language to build applications that could run on any interactive television, regardless of the underlying hardware that any individual unit had. Although Oak was not successful, it developed further into the Java 1.0 released by Sun Microsystems promising "Write Once, Run Anywhere" (WORA) code. This was a major innovation that arrived at a time where there was a demand for lower cost development capable of producing applications that could run in a range of machines, and on the fast-paced range of new web browsers that were emerging.

At the heart of this innovation was the idea of the Java Virtual Machine (JVM). The JVM was an abstract implementation of a general-purpose microprocessor, with a corresponding low-level byte code language specification. Although this abstract microprocessor did not actually exist, it was similar in design to the vast range of commercial microprocessors available, so the "last leg" translation of the JVM byte code to actual machine code for a specific microprocessor was a simple, speedy and low-cost task. Any Java compiler just needed to translate the Java source code to JVM bytecode, and the code could then execute on any device equipped with a JVM.

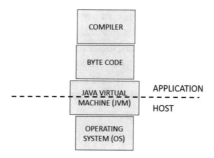

Software developers soon provided JVMs for all popular platforms. This idea of a virtual machine or "sand box" has been widely adopted in other software engineering applications and frameworks as it offers flexibility with very little loss of efficiency. It's how Macs can pretend to be PCs, and how systems can be built with components written in different languages.

Java received a particular boost resulting from the emergence of mobile computing platforms. Manufacturers of smartphone and tablet devices faced the same challenges as the earlier developers of interactive television set top boxes—the need to run the same code on different underlying devices. So, Java was a natural choice as the implementation language for the Android operating system (Google, 2007) and its applications.

Java has continued to evolve and was acquired by the Oracle Corporation following their acquisition of Sun Microsystems in 2010 and continues to be free to use. It is available as a run time only package (JRE) and as a development toolkit (JDK). As at 2018, Java is in version SE 11 and there is an Enterprise Edition EE 8 (known as Jakarta EE). A separate version of the JVM (Android Runtime and, before that, Dalvik) and a branch of the language exist for mobile development.

So, Java is a modern OO compiled language that relies on the virtual JVM for execution of its byte code. It owes its syntactic ancestry to C and draws on Smalltalk-80 for inspiration. It is, and has always been, free to use and embodies the "WORA" principle.

1.6 Tools of the Trade

To create Java programs, you will need to download some tools. They can all be downloaded from reputable sources for free:

- **The Java Development Kit (JDK)**: choose the latest version appropriate for your development machine. All major platforms are supported. For this book, we assume you are using a desktop development environment rather than a mobile platform. The JDK contains the Java compiler and several other tools to help you develop, debug and document your work. Ensure that your download the Java Development Kit (JDK) rather than the Run Time Environment (JRE)—your computer likely has the latter installed already.
- **An Integrated Development Environment (IDE)**: this is a toolset to help you edit and manage the code that you produce. There are many popular IDEs available. The professional market leaders are Eclipse and Netbeans which are rich in features, but overly complex for learning and teaching. This book, and

many others, uses the BlueJ IDE that can be freely downloaded for all major platforms. BlueJ was developed specifically for teaching and learning and offers just the right set of features to enable you to develop code easily.

All the code examples used in this book are available freely in the on-line package that accompanies this book.

With that knowledge, it's time to start writing some programs.

Procedural Programming Basics in Java

2

In Chap. 1 we learned some of the key concepts and terminology around programming. In this chapter it's time to jump in and start to create our first programs in Java using the BlueJ Integrated Development Environment (IDE). The first programs that we shall consider will be necessarily simple., and are intended to introduce the reader to the basic workflow necessary to write, compile, execute and debug a Java program, and to the elements of procedural programming that constitute core programming knowledge applicable not just to Java, but a wide range of other procedural and Object Oriented (OO) languages. At this stage, we will not focus on the OO elements of Java—that subject is explored in depth Chap. 3. Instead we shall master some basic procedural programming elements that make up an essential component of the broader landscape of coding.

2.1 First Program and Workflow

The traditional first program in many textbooks is "Hello World", so we shall start there. To create a Java program using BlueJ, first start the BlueJ program and under the Project menu tab select "New Project". Give the project a name. The project name will be used to create a directory on your PC/Mac. A BlueJ project is effectively a set of files contained within a directory. That set of files will ultimately consist of source code (.java files), compiled Java byte code (.class files) and other files that, taken together, constitute your Java application. Once you have done that you should have a screen that looks like this:

© Springer Nature Switzerland AG 2019
K. Sage, *Concise Guide to Object-Oriented Programming*,
Undergraduate Topics in Computer Science,
https://doi.org/10.1007/978-3-030-13304-7_2

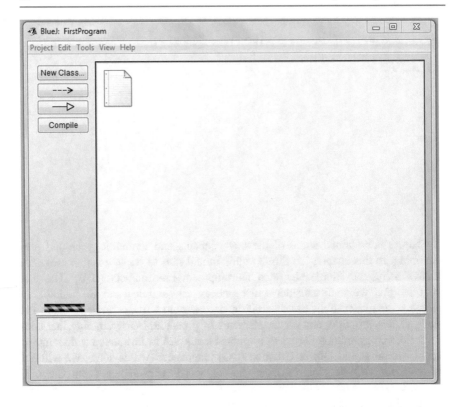

The precise appearance and layout may vary slightly depending on which version of BlueJ you have installed on your machine. There are some key controls to appreciate:

- **Menu bar**: where you will find key operations such as saving and opening projects.
- **Central panel**: the large panel on the top right where organisational chunks of code will ultimately be represented.
- **Workbench**: the panel at the bottom of the screen where you will be able to monitor your completed program as it executes.
- **The left-hand side key controls panel**: where you will find buttons to create a "New class" and "compile" your programs.

To create a Java program, the workflow is as follows:

- **Create a project**: A project is a collection of files that make up a program or application.
- **Create one or more "classes"**: A class is an organisational unit of a Java program. We shall consider this is much more depth in Chap. 3. For now, we just need to understand that a Java program is built from one or more

organisational units of functionality. At this stage we shall build a program from just one class, and that class will contain all the code that we need.

- **Compile the class into Java byte code**: this may require several attempts at editing the code using the BlueJ source code editor.
- **Create an instance of the class**: again, this terminology will become clearer in Chap. 3. For now, we can think of this as "creating a functioning incarnation of our program on the Java Virtual Machine".
- **Call a method**: summoning some aspect of the instance of the class to make the program "do something useful".
- **If there are problems, we may also need to go back and fix errors**: this is the process (some would say art) of "debugging".

So, we start by creating a class. To do this, press the "New Class" button on the left-hand panel. Your will be asked for a Class Name. Provide an alphanumeric name. By convention, Java classes start with a capital (upper case) letter. They should not start with a number, and there should not be any spaces in the name. Many experienced programmers use the "camel caps" style of naming where capital letters are used at the start of key words e.g. "MyFirstClass", or "My1st-Class". The Class Type should be left as "Class" and this is the BlueJ default. The BlueJ source code editor will open. Once you have done this an orange box will appear in the central panel with a hatched marking through it.

> A **class** (an organisational unit of a Java program) is represented in BlueJ by an orange box in the central panel. Double click on a class to invoke the BlueJ source code editor.
>
> If a class is shown with a hatched marking through it, then it has not yet been compiled into Java byte code. Pressing the **Compile** button will start that process.
>
> If a class is shown in solid orange, then it has been compiled successfully and is ready for use.

Note that BlueJ does produce some sample code when a class is created. This sample code is not particularly useful, so we will delete most of it. Just leave the skeleton of the class definition as shown below:

```
/**
 * Write a description of class MyFirstClass here.
 *
 * @author (your name)
 * @version (a version number or a date)
 */
public class MyFirstClass
{

}
```

Note carefully the type of curly brackets (often called "braces") that are used in the definition of the class. We will be making a great deal of use of two types of brackets:

- **Braces**: { and } used in the definition of chunks of code.
- **Round brackets**: (and) used in the definition of statements and method calls.

Now we will add some useful source code to make our first working program:

```java
/**
 * Write a description of class MyFirstClass here.
 *
 * @author Kingsley Sage
 * @version 1.0
 */

public class MyFirstClass
{
    public void myFirstMethod()
    {
        // This is a one-line comment.
        System.out.println("Hello World");
    }
}
```

This example is a complete definition of the MyFirstClass class. The class definition is contained within a pair of braces. Everything inside that pair of braces is a part of the class definition. To help us remember what we are doing, we add comments to our source code. Comments do not form part of the compiled byte code—they are there for our benefit, and for the benefit of others reading our code. Comments come in two types.

> **Multi line comments**: starting with the symbol pair /* and ending with the symbol pair */. Any text can appear between those pairs and can run over many lines. Here we have used a multi-line comment to provide information about who has written the program.
>
> **Single line comments**: start with the symbol pair //. Any text after this symbol pair up to the end of the line are treated as text comments.

Inside the class definition we have a public method called myFirstMethod(). A method is one of the component parts of a class definition and represents something that the class can do (a behaviour). If you have previous experience of procedural programming (e.g. using C) you will recognise this as the concept of a function (however there is a difference between a function and a method that we explore in Chap. 3). Note that by convention method names start with a lower-case letter so that we can easily distinguish them from classes. Note also that the method has a pair of round brackets after it.

In the case of both the class and the class' method definitions, the keyword `public` simply means that the functionality is openly accessible. We will return to the importance of the keyword `void` later when we delve further into the concept of a method.

`System.out.println()` is a pre-defined library method that displays text on the console. As we have not created any kind of Graphical User Interface (GUI), our output will be simple text on the console window. BlueJ will cause the console window to open as required when we execute the code. You will notice that `System` starts with a capital letter. This is because it refers to a class.

The `System` class is a programmatic representation of the Java Virtual Machine. As Java was created as a platform independent language, it does not readily provide any means of addressing the underlying hardware that your program is running is running on.

If you need to communicate with the host PC, for example to display something on the screen, or open a file, you do so by interacting with the `System` class. There is only ever one `System` object, and you do not need to do anything to bring it into existence. You can think of the `System` object as a proxy for the JVM.

The final thing to note is the semi-colon at the end of a line of code. This marks the end of a complete statement of Java code, a bit like the full stop that we put at the end of a sentence when writing in English.

If you have written everything correctly, you can now press the Compile button and the source code will be translated into Java byte code. If you have made an error, the compiler will produce an error message (a syntax error) and you will need to fix the problem and try to compile again. When the source code is free from syntax errors and compiled, you will see the message "Class compiled—no syntax errors". Now it's time to run our first program. To run the program, you will need to create an instance of `MyFirstClass`. To do this, right click the solid orange box on the central panel and select new `MyFirstClass`. You can then give the instance of the class a name. Just use the default name for now. Once you have done that you a red box will appear on the BlueJ workbench.

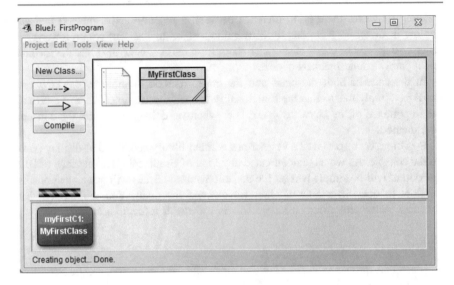

The red box is a Java object built from the MyFirstClass class definition.

A Java class is a definition of an organisational unit of a Java program. They appear as orange boxes on the BlueJ central panel.

A Java object is an instance of a Java class. An object is "instantiated" from a Java class. We can instantiate many Java objects from the same Java class definition.

Now that we have created a Java object, we have a functioning program working in the memory of our machine. Now all we need to do is to tell the object what we want to do. The object only has one thing that it can do. We need to invoke the myFirstMethod() chunk of code. To do this, we right click on the object on the workbench and select the void myFirstMethod(). This will cause the console window to open and your message will appear. Well done, you have created and executed your first Java program!

2.2 Primitive Data Types

Now that we have looked at the basic workflow for creating and executing a Java program, we can now delve deeper into the basics of the procedural aspects of programming. Our first program just displayed some text on the console window. More useful programs will do rather more, and in particular, will allow us to store and manipulate data. By data, we mean any type of information including, although not limited to, numeric data, logical data, text and objects. We can view the purpose of a program as a means of doing some useful work on data.

Data is stored in the form or variables. We start by considering the most basic kind of data, called "primitive data". The term "primitive" here is used to distinguish between data that is atomic (in the sense that it cannot be broken down into any smaller useful units) and that does not have the status of an object, and objects. We consider much more about objects in Chap. 3. Java has 8 primitive types in total, 6 for numeric data, 1 for single character data and 1 for logical or `boolean` expressions. Each is characterised by a range of values that a variable of that type can hold and the number of bytes in memory that it occupies. The 8 primitive types are:

Type	Description	Size	Example value
boolean	True or false	1 bit	true, false
byte	Integer	1 byte (8 bits)	
char	Unicode character	2 bytes	'a', '\u0030'
short	Integer	2 bytes	−3, −2, −5
int	Integer	4 bytes	−3, −2, −5
long	Integer	8 bytes	−3L, 0L, 4L
float	Floating point	4 bytes	1.2f, −1.2e03f
double	Floating point	8 bytes	1.2, −1.2e03

The choice of integer and floating-point types simply reflects the range of values that each type can accommodate. In Java, all numeric types are signed, meaning that they can take on positive and negative values (there is no distinction between signed and unsigned types as there is in languages such as C).

Primitive data is stored in the form of variables. To use a variable we must declare it first. This ensures that the compiler knows how much memory to set aside to store each variable. Java is a strongly typed language, meaning that we must always state what kind of data something is before we can use it. This declaration happens only once. We can store values in the variables and manipulate those values as our needs dictate. Note that the primitive data type keywords start with lower case letters to remind us that they do not have the status of a class. Primitive variables also have default values (0 for the numeric ones and `false` for `boolean` ones).

Here are some example of primitive variables being declared and then given some values:

```
int x;
boolean y;
double x1;
float x2;
char myLetter;

x = 3;
y = true;
x1 = 1.5;
x2 = 6.5f;
myLetter = 'x';
```

You can also combine a declaration with setting an initial value:

```
int x = 3;
boolean y = false;
```

You can manipulate variable values using an expression. Here are some examples of valid expressions using a range of mathematical operators.

```
x = 5;
x = x + 2;    // Add 2 to the value of x

int z = 2;
x = z + 2;

x += 4;       // Add 4 to the value of x
x++;          // Increase x by 1
x--;          // Decrease x by 1

x = x * 6;    // Multiply x by 6
x = x / 2;    // Integer divide x by 2

y = false;
x2 = x2 / 5.2f;
```

For an expression, the right-hand side of the equals sign is evaluated and used to set the variable on the left-hand side. Many programmers do not care for the $x = x + 2$ way of writing "add two to 2" as it resembles an impossible equation. But in practice it does not matter—just use a style that works for you. Note that all expressions end with the semi-colon. You can also see the quite popular "side style" of commenting.

Variables must be declared before they are used. Failure to do so will result in the compiler reporting an error. However, it is important to understand that where we place the declarations of variables determines their "ownership" under the "rules of scope". Variables can be declared within the scope of a class, or within an individual method, or indeed part of a method. The first two cases are relevant at this stage.

A variable that is declared within the class definition, but outside the scope of any method within that class is referred to (interchangeably) as an **instance variable**, a **class attribute**, and a **field of a class**. However, the term "class variable" is not appropriate. We shall see in a later chapter that class variable refers to something different. Such a variable is accessible at any point in the source code within that class. We say that it has **scope of the class**.

A variable that is declared within an individual method within a class definition is referred to a **method variable**. It is accessible only within the code for that method. When the method is not actively executing, the variable cannot be accessed and does not exist. We say that it has the **scope of the method**.

Unlike other programming languages, there is no concept in Java of a global variable. All variables must belong to some organisational unit of your program. We can use built in methods such as `System.out.println()` to display the current value of any variable in the console window. Here is an example method that does exactly that:

```
public void useVariables()
{
    int a;
    int b =2;
    double c;
    double d = 4.5;
    double e;
    a = 2;
    a++;
    c = -4.5;
    e = c * d;
    System.out.println("a multiplied by b is " + a * b);
    System.out.println("The value of e is " + e);
}
```

Note the use of the + symbol in the call to `System.out.println()`. Here the + symbol is called the "concatenation operator". Concatenation simply means to place one thing after another

2.3 The Procedural Programming Paradigm

Now that we know about the primitive data types, we turn our attention to the fundamental concepts of procedural programming. Java is an Object Oriented language, but it also has the procedural programming concepts as its core, as do many other programming languages. The term "procedural programming" is not entirely well-defined, and is contentious for some academics. In the broadest terms, it refers to a style of programming where a problem is broken down in a set of smaller procedures, also called functions and, in Java's case, methods. But the term is also used to include a set of programming code constructions (structured programming) that deliver the minimal requirements of a general-purpose programming language.

These constructions themselves arise from the pioneering work of Alan Turing and his abstract Turing machine mentioned in Chap. 1.

Rather than dwell on the detailed mathematical treatments that many purists attach to programming paradigms, we will instead describe what is required of a general-purpose programming language in rather more everyday terms. Suffice to say that it can be demonstrated that a programming language is general purpose (i.e. can perform any computable calculation) provided it exhibits 3 characteristics:

- **Sequence**: processes one instruction after another, until all instructions have been executed.
- **Alternation (also called selection)**: selects one execution path from a set of alternatives.
- **Repetition (also called iteration)**: repeatedly executes some code whilst some condition persists.

All general-purpose languages exhibit these three characteristics. They may do so in different ways, and they may have other features besides. But these other features are present only to make the language easier to use, and they are not actually a pre-requisite for the language being general purpose. As Java is a general-purpose programming language, it provides (a variety of) means of delivering these core characteristics.

2.4   Sequence

The notion of sequence from structured programming is simply the idea that instructions are executed in a given reliable order i.e. from start to finish. It is up to the programmer to determine what the correct sequence is to achieve the intended result. This idea contrasts with the concept of declarative programming, where the user simply states what their requirements are, and the order of these declarative statements is unimportant.

The only additional aspect of sequence comes from the procedural programming paradigm, that adds the notion of a "call stack". This reflects the idea that a larger program can be broken down int smaller pieces—methods in the case of Java. One method can then call upon another. This is also the concept behind the program design philosophy of "task decomposition" where a large task is broken down into a set of smaller tasks, until each task is sufficiently simple to be understood and implemented.

When a method calls upon another method, execution of the calling method is parked whilst the called method is executed. Once the called method has completed execution, control passes back to the calling method. At any stage of the execution of the program, there is a stack of calling methods where the order of the stack is determined by the sequence in which the method calls took place. The following example will help you understand this point:

```
public void method1()
{
    int x=2;
    int y=3;
    method2();
    System.out.println("Value of y in method1 is: " + y);
}

public void method2()
{
    boolean x = true;
    int y=6;
    System.out.println("x is: " + x);
    System.out.println("Value of y in method2 is: " + y);
    method3();
}

public void method3()
{
    int y = 5;
    System.out.println("Value of y in method3 is: " + y);
}
```

Let's imagine that we invoke method1(). We see that method1() does some work, then calls method2(). This parks method1() on the call stack and method2() starts to execute. Then method2() calls method3(), parking method2() on the call stack. Next, method3() finishes and control passes back to method2(). We then see that method2() finishes, and control passes back to method1(). Finally, method1() finishes. Note that in this example the variable y is used in all three methods. But y is a method variable, so the version in method1() is unique to that method, and distinct from the y used in method2() and so on. In general, *__what goes inside the method, stays in the method__*.

We can visualise a call stack as follows:

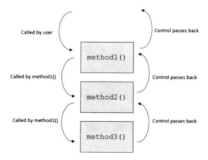

We shall see later that as well as passing control from one method to another, we can pass and return values as well.

2.5 Alternation

The next element from structured programming to understand is alteration (also known as selection). Alternation is concerned with selecting an execution path from a set of possible alternatives i.e. making a choice. That choice will depend on some decision criteria, and only one of the possible alternatives can be pursued i.e. the choices are mutually exclusive. We can use a simple flowchart diagram to illustrate the concept:

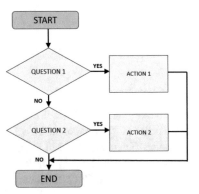

Here we see that we are required to evaluate a question. This question has a `boolean` nature in that the answer can only be either "yes" (`true`) or "no" (`false`). If the answer to question 1 is `true`, we perform action 1. If the answer to question 1 is `false`, we instead evaluate question 2. If the answer to question 2 is `false`, we perform action 2. Note that is question 1 was `true`, we never evaluated question 2, so the two questions here have answers that are mutually exclusive. We could have carried on extending the chain of questions as long as we liked. But once we find a question that evaluates to `true`, the decision-making process is complete.

Alternation in Java (as in many other languages) is delivered using `if` and `switch` statements. They are both equally expressive in that anything that is written using `switch` can be re-written using `if`. There are situations where it is aesthetically more pleasing to use one over another, but this is a choice for the programmer.

The `if` statement takes the general form:

```
if (<test-condition-1>)
   {
   // Body of statement
   }

else if (<test-condition-2>)
   {
   // Body of statement
   }

else
   {
   // Body of statement
   }
```

Note carefully the use of brackets here. The test conditions are contained in round brackets, and the body of the statement (the code that is to be executed if the test condition is true) is contained in braces. Note also that there is no semi-colon at the end of the test condition code.

We can have as many `else ... if` sections as we like, or none at all. We also have the option of having a final `else` section for an action to be performed when no other test expression in the statement overall evaluated as `true`. The test conditions are evaluated as either `true` or `false`. Such expressions will make use of Java operators. An operator is just a name for a symbol that performs a specific operation on one, two or three operands and returns a result. For example, + the addition symbol is an operator in the sense that 2 + 3 has two operands and returns the result 5. For the if statement, we will use operators that return values of true or false. The commonplace ones in this application are:

Operator	Meaning
==	Is equal to
!=	Is not equal to
>	Is greater than
>=	Is greater than or equal to
<	Is less than
<=	Is less than or equal to
&&	Logical AND
||	Logical OR

Note the use of == as the equality operator. A common mistake in learning to code is to confuse the assignment operator = with the == equality operator. The assignment operator sets a variable to a specific value. The equality operator tests to see whether two values are the same or not.

The logical operators are used to combine tests together to make more complex test conditions that depend on two or more pieces of data. Logical AND only evaluates as true if all sub-conditions evaluate as true. Logical OR evaluates as true if any of the sub-conditions evaluates as true.

Here are some example if statements:

```java
int a = 1;
int b = 2;
int c = 3;
boolean x = true;

// Example 1
if (a == 1)
{
    System.out.println("Get here if a has the value 1");
}

// Example 2
if (a != 1)
{
    System.out.println("a does not have the value 1");
}

// Example 3
if (a > 2)
{
    System.out.println("a has a value greater than 2");
}
else
{
    System.out.println("Otherwise we get here!");
}

// Example 4
if ((a==1) && (x == true))
{
    System.out.println("a is 1 AND x is true");
}
```

The switch statement provides an alternative means of expressing our alternation needs. A switch statement makes use of a single variable to determine which of the options is to be executed. Each option is characterised by a case statement, and each case should end with a break statement. The break statement is used to denote that the end of the switch has been reached, and that no further options need to be considered. There is no particular advantage in using switch over if, but it is worth noting that there are fewer brackets in the switch coding (just the one set of braces for the for the switch as a whole), but the decision making is limited to just a single variable, unlike if statements that can use logical operators to build up more complex decision making criteria. The `default` case functions like a final `else` option for an `if` statement and provides a reliable course of execution when no other valid `switch` option is found. Here is an example of a `switch` statement:

```
int x = 3;

switch(x)
{
    case 1:
        System.out.println("Option if x has the value 1");
        break;
    case 2:
        System.out.println("Option if x has the value 2");
        break;
    case 3:
        System.out.println("Option if x has the value 3");
        break;
    default:
        System.out.println("x has some other value");
        break;
}
```

2.6 Repetition

Repetition (also called iteration) is concerned with situations where a program needs to repeatedly execute some portion of code whilst some condition persists. This is also commonly referred to as the concept of "looping" and programmers will often describe such code fragments as program loops. The origin of the term loop is easy to appreciate when we use a simple flowchart to illustrate the generic concept. The flowchart forms a closed loop that we iterate around a number of times:

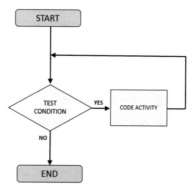

Repetition in the Java language is delivered using for, while and do ..
while loops. As before, there is no real difference in expressive power between
these loop constructions and it is down to the programmer to choose the loop style
that is most appropriate in any particular scenario.

The for loop takes the following general form:

```
for (<initial-state>; <test-condition>; <action>)
{
     // Body of loop
}
```

We see that three things need to be specific in the round brackets:

- The **<initial-state>**: the initial value of some controlling variable that we will be
  set one-time prior to the first evaluation of the test condition to some initial
  value.
- The **<test-condition>**: a boolean test that will determine whether the loop
  continues to execute.,
- The **<action>**: a short section of code that is executed each time the body of the
  loop has finished executing.

The body of the loop is any amount of valid Java code (including, although not
limited to, sequence, alternation and other examples of repetition).

The for loop is most easily understood using a code example together with a
specific companion flowchart as shown below:

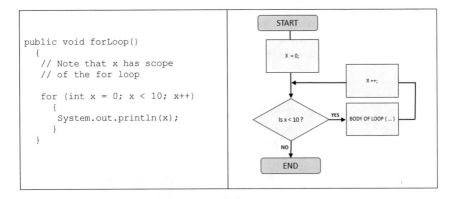

Note here that the loop variable x was actually declared within the scope of the
for loop. It therefore has the scope of just that loop, and does not exist outside
the scope of the loop. This is a common practice in coding. It does not have to be
the case, you could declare the loop variable as a method variable, or use an
instance variable. It simply depends on whether you will need access to the loop

variable once the loop has completed execution. In this example, the result of calling this method would be to print out the values 0 to 9 inclusive on the console window.

A common error for first time coders is to mistakenly add a semi-colon to the end of the `for` loop round brackets like this:

```
for (int x = 0; x < 10; x++);
  {
    System.out.println(x);
  }
```

This would not actually be syntactically valid. The semi-colon is the smallest body of a statement you can have in Java. So here, the body is assumed to be blank and nothing is executed in respect of it. The braces are then entered, and we try to access the value of x, but x is now out of scope. It does not matter that there are excess braces.

As an alternative to the for lop construction, we can use the `while` loop. The general form of the `while` loop is simpler than the `for` loop:

```
while (<test-condition>)
{
    // Body of loop
}
```

Here we see that there is just a simple `boolean` test condition. If the test condition evaluates as `true`, we enter the body of the loop. Once the body of the loop has completed executing, the test condition is evaluated again. The body of the loop is repeatedly executed until the test condition evaluates as `false`.

As before, the `while` loop is most easily understood using a code example together with a specific companion flowchart as shown below:

```
public void whileLoop()
  {
    // q has scope of the method
    int q = 5;

    while (q > 0)
      {
        System.out.println(q);
        q++;
      }
  }
```

Note that in this example, the declaration and initialisation of the loop variable q does not form a part of the while loop itself. It is also important to realise that it is the programmer's responsibility to ensure that something within the body of the while loop affects the loop variable so that the loop can ultimately exit. In this case it's the q++; statement. Failure to do so would result in the loop executing forever (an "infinite loop"). If this eventuality, the JVM will need to be reset manually. The BlueJ IDE has a control for this—depending on which version you have installed it may be a "barbers' pole" or a circular arrow. In either case, just right click the control and reset the JVM.

It is easy to see that any code written in the form of a for loop can be re-written in the form of a while loop. The only real advantage of the while loop is that the for loop action is limited to just one simple statement of code, typically incrementing/decrementing the loop variable. With the while loop, you can incorporate as much action style code into the body of the loop as is required to solve a problem.

The final form of repetition for now is the rather less used do ... while loop. This loop takes the following general form:

```
do
{
     // Body of loop
}
while (<test-condition>)
```

Once again, the do .. while loop is most easily understood using a code example together with a specific companion flowchart as shown below:

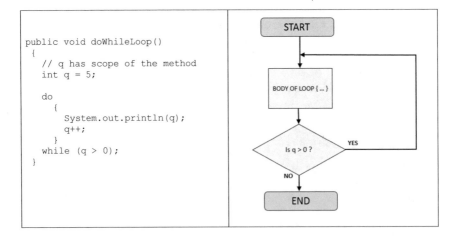

```
public void doWhileLoop()
{
    // q has scope of the method
    int q = 5;

    do
      {
         System.out.println(q);
         q++;
      }
    while (q > 0);
}
```

Here we see that the test condition is positioned after the body of the loop. This means that the `boolean` test condition is not evaluated until after the body of the loop has been executed for the first time. This means that the body of the loop is guaranteed to be executed at least once, even if the test condition should turn out to be `false`. This loop is often used in the context of user interfaces and user interaction, where a user needs to input some value before the value can be determined as acceptable or not. If the value is not within some acceptable bounds, the loop runs again to invite the user to try again.

2.7 More on Methods

We have previously discussed methods as a component part of a class definition that detail what a class can "do" (behaviours). It is now appropriate to dig deeper into the nature of methods, as we shall be using them extensively from this point onwards.

Methods have their origins in the mathematical concept of a function. Perhaps that is unsurprising as many early pioneers of computer science were themselves mathematicians. Without having to resort to any detailed maths, we can characterise a method as follows:

> A **method** is a function that belongs to a class. A method performs some useful behaviour made up using code. A method can have any number of inputs, and either one or zero output. A method with zero outputs is called a **void method**.

We can visual the concept of a method in two ways:

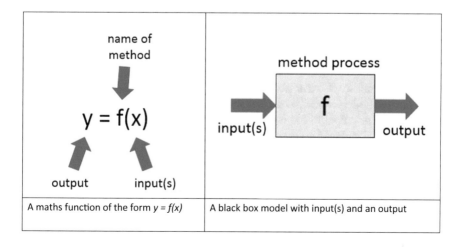

| A maths function of the form $y = f(x)$ | A black box model with input(s) and an output |

The maths way is helpful is it helps us understand the origins of the syntax for calling methods. The black box model is helpful as it reminds us of the procedural programming paradigm, and the fact that the process inside the method is encapsulated within that method.

All methods in Java must belong to a class—they cannot exist in isolation. They can be defined anywhere inside their host class. A method definition takes the general form:

```
<access-modifier> <return-type> method-name(<formal-parameters>)
{
    // Body of method
    <return-statement-if-not-void>
}
```

In summary:

- **<Access-modifier>**: `public` or **`private`** depending on whether the method is intended to be invokable by other classes, or only by methods inside the class in which it was defined. Other access modifiers also exist. If not specified, the access modifier is assumed to be `public`.
- **<return-type>**: the Java type of any output generated by this method. If the method does not produce any returned output, the return type is `void`. A return type must always be specified.
- **The method-name**: any valid name, by convention starting with a lower-case letter.
- **The <formal-parameters>**: a list of zero or more parameters that the method will take as inputs to do the job that is designed to perform. If there are no inputs, the set of empty round brackets must still be included to denote that this is a method definition.
- **return statement:** if the method produces a value to be returned, i.e. it is not `void`, then the `return` statement is used to signify the value that is returned. Executing a `return` statement at any point during a method invocation causes the method to finish.

It is important to be clear about the nature of output or returned values. Just because a method is `void`, does not mean it cannot do something useful. For example, writing output to the console is not considered an output in a functional sense. In pure functional programming languages (such as Haskell), functions are not permitted to exhibit such "side effects" but in Java methods may produce such side effects. This is very useful in using methods to support the task decomposition coding principle.

Here is an example method definition that takes two formal parameters and produces an output:

```
public int addTwoNumbers(int a, int b)
{
    int c;
    c = a + b;
    return c;
}
```

To use this method, we would use some calling code (within another method) like this:

```
int d;
d = addTwoNumbers(3,4);
System.out.println(d);
```

In this example, we invoke the method addTwoNumbers() with two actual parameters, 3 and 4 in this case. This matches the formal parameter list in the method definition, that stated the method expected two int parameters as inputs. The first parameter is then assigned the variable a inside the scope of the method definition, and the second is assigned the variable b. The variable c is a method variable. The addTwoNumbers() method then does some useful work in its inputs (Adding them in this case) and then returns the value c. That value is then assigned to the int variable d in the calling code. If we tried to invoke addTwoNumbers() with only one parameter, the compiler would display an error, as the undertaking was to provide two int numbers. Our definition also gave an undertaking to return one int to the calling code. This was achieved using the return keyword. If we forgot the return keyword in the method definition, the compiler would have also identified an error.

Here is another example of a method that takes two parameters, determines which is larger and displays an appropriate message on the console:

```
public void showLarger(int a, int b)
{
    if (a > b)
    {
        System.out.println("a is larger");
    }
    else if (b > a)
    {
        System.out.println("b is larger");
    }
    else
    {
        System.out.println("a is equal to b");
    }
}
```

Note that as this method is void, there is no return keyword. But the method does exhibit side effects, displaying messages on the console.

2.8 Bringing It All Together

We are now able to start to create some more substantive and interesting programs. To consolidate the principles learned this far, we now consider a simple and complete game. The game is a version of the "guess the number I am thinking of". The rules of the game are:

- The program will generate a random number in the range 1–99 (inclusive).
- The user will have up to 10 attempts to guess the number.
- If the number guessed is too low, a "too low" message is displayed on console.
- If the number guess is too high, a "too high" message is displayed on console.
- The game ends if the user guesses correctly, or has had 10 attempts.

The only code that needs to be added to our existing knowledge base is the means to generate a random number and the means to allow the user to enter a number at the console. This functionality is achieved here using the Java library Random and Scanner classes respectively. Don't worry if these are the only two aspects of the code example given here that you are unsure about—as library classes, their operation will become clearer in later chapters. Here is the complete code listing for the guessing game:

```java
import java.util.*;

/**
 * A simple guessing game.
 *
 * @author Kingsley Sage
 * @version 1.0
 */

public class GuessingGame
{
    // Instance variables
    private int answer;
    // Initialise the scanner for user input
    Scanner sc = new Scanner(System.in);

    public void playGame()
    {
        // Initialise the random answer
        Random r = new Random();
        answer = r.nextInt(99)+1;

        int numGuesses;
        boolean gameOver = false;
        int userGuess;
        numGuesses = 0;

        // The main game loop
        while (gameOver == false)
        {
            userGuess = getGuessFromUser();
            analyseGuess(userGuess);
            numGuesses++;

            if (numGuesses > 10)
            {
                System.out.println("Out of guesses!");
                System.out.println("The answer was " + answer);
```

```
                        gameOver = true;
                }
                else if (answer == userGuess)
                {
                        gameOver = true;
                }
        }
    }

    private int getGuessFromUser()
    {
        int x;
        System.out.println("Enter your guess: ");
        x = sc.nextInt(); // Fetches an int from the console
        return x;
    }

    private void analyseGuess(int guess)
    {
        if (guess > answer)
        {
            System.out.println("Too high");
        }
        else if (guess < answer)
        {
            System.out.println("Too low");
        }
        else
        {
            System.out.println("Well done!");
        }
    }
}
```

To play the game, just create an instance of the GuessingGame class in BlueJ and call the method playGame(). This code has been created to demonstrate the ideas that have been discussed in this chapter. There are several points worthy of note:

- The import statement at the top draws in additional Java functionality, in this case the library (a part of the extended Java code landscape) that includes the Random and Scanner classes.
- Only the playGame() method is public. That is because it is the only method that is intended for the user to call directly. The playGame() method calls upon two other methods, but they are declared private as they are only intended to be called within the class definition, and have no utility beyond the class definition.
- The Java Random number generator generates values in the range 0 to an upper limit (exclusive of the value of the upper limit). We want a value in the range 1 to 99 inclusively, so we add 1 to the number generated.

- There is no validation of the numbers entered by the user in the `getGuessFromUser()` method. This could be added conveniently using a `do ... while` loop (left to the reader as an exercise).

This game should serve to illustrate many of the core programming concepts in action. Now that you understand those basics, it is time to expand our thinking to embrace the Object Oriented design philosophy fully. Out code up to this point has been based upon a single class. Although that was useful for understanding coding basics, it has not made any use of the much broader power of OO, and that is where we turn our attention for the next chapter.

Getting into Object Oriented Programming

3

In Chap. 1, we considered why OO has become such a cornerstone of modern software development. It helps us to develop programs in a structured manner that mirrors some real-world problem. In this chapter we expand on this core idea and see how we can reflect the real world using OO design, and then go on to create some simple multi class programs in Java. In doing so we will master some essential OO terminology. As well as considering code, we also spend some time exploring the key related, but not directly coding dependent, activity of OO design. As we shall see, OO design and OO coding are not two distinct activities (at least they shouldn't be) and the key to good coding starts with a proper understanding of the structure of the problem you want to solve.

3.1 Object Oriented in a Social Context

One of the easiest ways of getting insight into the OO concept is to consider how things in our everyday experience are organised. Many of us will work in offices, play team sports, go shopping and make plans to go on holiday. These tasks seem normal to us and very much in the domain of our experience. Although you might not spend much time thinking about them, all these activities are underpinned by structure. Some of this is social structure, such as the management structures in our workplace, or the organisation of sports teams or the interactions between a complex set of businesses and people that allow us to book holidays in distant places. In fact, part of the human experience is that we readily organise into social structures to achieve tasks collectively. OO design and coding allows us to reflect that structure when we produce a piece of software. We can understand the principles of OO design just by reflecting on these social structures.

Consider a modern office that delivers some service. It doesn't matter what that service is, but for the sake of this example, let's imagine that the service is IT telephone support. Let's say that the office has several different categories of employees:

© Springer Nature Switzerland AG 2019
K. Sage, *Concise Guide to Object-Oriented Programming*,
Undergraduate Topics in Computer Science,
https://doi.org/10.1007/978-3-030-13304-7_3

- **Telephone operator**: who takes the calls and routes them to first line support staff.
- **First line supports staff**: who deal with the most straightforward problems and determine whether more complex problems need to be referred to second line support staff.
- **Second line support staff**: who have deep technical expertise and produce advice for more complex cases.
- **IT support staff**: who keep the internal desktop systems and the telephones running in an orderly manner.
- **Team leaders:** who manage staff and ensure that their working conditions are appropriate.
- **HR staff**: who ensure that everybody gets paid the correct amount for the work that they do.
- **Cleaners**: who ensure that the working environment is kept up to the required standard.

We could go on, but you get the idea. There are many different types of staff, and they all have a particular specialism and expertise, and they are all necessary for the efficient and effective conduct of the business. The organisation seems reasonable in our experience. But how does the business actually operate? To help us understand that, we could draw a diagram.

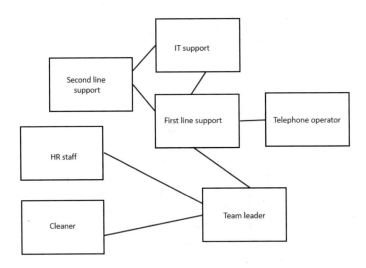

The diagram is interesting as it reveals some of the structure of this business. Each link in the diagram represents a channel of communication between two organisational units of the business. That link could be a telephone, an email link, but it represents an interaction. The telephone operators exchange messages with the first line support staff, but not the second line support staff. The cleaning staff receive their instructions from the team leaders. The team leaders need to communicate and interact with the HR staff. OK, there may be other links, but the diagram is capturing the essence of the interactions between the organisational units of the business. It's just the way the business is supposed to work. From this simple model, we can extract some useful general observations about what makes this business work:

- Each organisational unit has a single specific purpose. That purpose can be clearly and simply expressed.
- Each organisational unit has a need for information. Some of it is needed solely for its own use, and some it may need to share with other organisational units.
- Each organisational unit has a need to interact with one or more other units in order to achieve some collective task.

These same principles underpin the concept of OO design. We just need to apply particular terms to each of these ideas.

3.2   Introducing the OO Class

In the previous chapter, we saw the term "class", but did not give any consideration to its meaning. Now we can establish a useful definition:

A **class** is an organisational unit of an Object Oriented design and program.

A key task in producing an OO design and program is therefore the identification and selection of the most appropriate organisational units. There is no single OO solution for any specific problem, there are just "good" ones and everything else. So we need to establish a set of principles that will help us understand what makes for a "good" choice of an organisational unit or class. We will find that if we choose wisely, our programming task is relatively straightforward. Choose poorly, and our software may be difficult to deliver, hard to maintain and ultimately not a useful solution to our problem - just like an office with poor internal organisation. We can draw on our analysis from the previous section. A good class would exhibit the following characteristics:

Highly cohesive: the class represents a single useful entity or organisational unit and does that job well.

Minimally coupled: the class limits its interactions with other classes to only those that are really necessary for it to do what it is designed to do.

Encapsulation: the class keeps information necessary to its internal operation private and does not expose it to other classes, and only makes public the information necessary for it to interact with other classes in the intended manner.

It should be noted these characteristics are design aspirations, and not an absolute manifesto. There will be occasions where these ideals are difficult to realise completely, but we should be guided by them.

In our office example, a telephone operator is exactly that. There is a clear well-defined notion of an entity (or "thing"). It is distinct from, say, a first line support staff member. But it will have interactions with that staff member, but they are limited in nature, essentially to passing on a message from a customer and logging a call. The telephone operator has no operational need of communication with the second line support staff. So the telephone operator seems to aspire to the idea of high cohesion and low or minimal coupling. The telephone operator will have some information about them that is necessary for them to function correctly, such as the amount of time since they last had a coffee, or how much money they have in their pocket to buy that coffee. But no-one else in the office has any operational need to know that information, so they keep it private. But other information, such as long they have been on shift, does need to be shared with other staff members to allow the office to be managed. So that information is public. So we also start to see the characterisation of data as private versus public and this underpins the notion of encapsulation.

So whenever we want to create an OO program, we should give thought to the notion of OO design and think about what classes or entities we need to create, using the principles of high cohesion, low coupling and encapsulation as our guide.

3.3 The Anatomy of a Class

Now we are at a point where we can start to build a more formal definition of a class in Java. In a general sense, any "thing", "entity" or "class" (these words are often used interchangeably in many books and articles) can be defined by two key components:

The things that they "are" (the **state**)
The things that they "do" (the **behaviour**)

Many formal OO design tools use techniques that analyse free text to derive state and behaviour by virtue of their presence as nouns (descriptive words) and verbs (action words). In a general sense everything can be defined this way. For example, take the following piece of text:

A sports car can be one of a variety of colours, with an engine power between 100 HP and 200 HP. It can be a convertible or a regular model. The car has a button that starts the engine and a parking brake. When the parking brake is released and you press the accelerator, it drives in the direction determined by the transmission setting.

We can break the car entity into state and behaviour as follows:

State	Behaviour
Colour (text)	Press the start button
Engine power (number of BHP)	Press the accelerator
Convertible? (yes/no)	
Parking brake (on/off)	

You can apply this kind of textual analysis to anything, from the telephone operator in our office example, to a car, to a football player character in a video game, a shopping cart in an e-commerce example and so on. It's a universal concept of defining what we mean by a "thing". And that gives us a template that we can use to define a class in an OO language. So let's take the car example and create a Java class that can model the car "entity" for us:

```java
/**
 * A simple class to represent a sports car
 *
 * @author Kingsley Sage
 * @version 1.0
 */

public class Car
{
    // Variables to describe the state ...

    String colour;
    double enginePower;
    boolean isConvertible;
    boolean isDirectionForwards;
    boolean parkingBrakeOn;
    boolean isMoving;
    boolean engineStarted;

    // Some methods to define the behaviour ...

    // A simple constructor method first ...

    public Car(String colour, double enginePower, boolean isConvertible)
    {
        this.colour = colour;
        this.enginePower = enginePower;
        this.isConvertible = isConvertible;
        isDirectionForwards = true;
        parkingBrakeOn = true;
        isMoving = false;
        engineStarted = false;
    }

    // Some other useful methods ...

    public void pressAccelerator()
    {
        if ((!parkingBrakeOn)&&(engineStarted))
        {

            System.out.println("The " + colour + " car is moving");
            isMoving = true;
        }
        else if (engineStarted)
        {
            System.out.println("The parking brake for the " + colour
                + " car is on!");
            isMoving = false;
        }
        else
        {
            System.out.println("The engine for the " + colour +
                " car is not started!");
        }
    }

    public void pressStartButton()
    {
        if (!engineStarted)
        {
            System.out.println("Engine for the " + colour +
                " car is starting");
            engineStarted = true;
        }
    }
}
```

So a Java class defines state as a set of variables that represents all the useful data needed, and the behaviour as a set of functions that represent all the things that it can do. For readers with previous procedural programming experience outside of OO, it is worth just making the distinction between a function (a block of code intended to be used repeatedly) and a method (a member function or "method" that is a function that belongs to a specific class). So our Java class has data and methods. In fact, Java is a pure OO language in that all code must belong to a class. This differentiates it from other OO languages, notably C++ where code can exist independently of classes or be structured in the form of classes, and any mix of the two approaches. So C++ can have both functions and methods. All functions in Java are necessarily methods as they must belong to a class, so we shall always use the term "method" from now onwards.

Now that we have a class, we can use BlueJ to bring it to life. At this point we need to make a very important distinction between the terms "class" and "object". When we create the Car class in BlueJ, we do so using the integrated text editor. The class appears as an orange rectangle. When we right click the class and select the "new" option, we get a red square on the BlueJ workbench. That red square is an object. So we have an important distinction:

A **class** is a template for some useful entity defined by its state and behaviour. It is not a specific example of that entity—it is blueprint for all instances of that entity. At the code level, there is only ever one definition of any class.

An **object** is a specific incarnation or instance of a class. It is a concrete occurrence of that class. There can be many instances of a class in existence at the same time.

So we have one Car class definition, and using BlueJ, we can make as make instances of that Car as we like. Just like in the office example, we can have a job description for a telephone operator and then use that description to hire as many actual concrete telephone operators as we need for the business to function properly.

So in BlueJ, we can use the Car class to make two objects car1 and car2. The objects can have any name we like provided they are unique. Note that by convention, only classes begin with an uppercase letter. Variables, methods (with one exception we shall note shortly) and objects (with an exception we shall note later) start with a lower-case letter. Java does not enforce this convention on us, but we should adopt this convention as it is good programming practice.

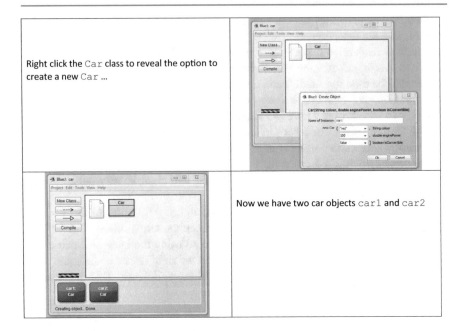

Right click the `Car` class to reveal the option to create a new `Car` …	
	Now we have two car objects `car1` and `car2`

Once we have created these two objects, we can inspect them using the BlueJ inspector. To use the inspector, just right click on the object on the BlueJ workbench and select "inspect":

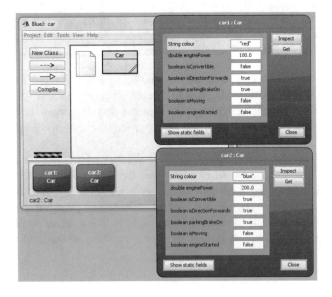

Note that in both cases, when we created ("instantiated") the two Car objects, BlueJ opened a dialog box and asked us for the values of three instance variables. This is down to the role of the constructor method. In the code you will see that there is a method that shares the precise same name as the class itself (Car in this case). Also note that the capitalisation is the name as the class name. This method name convention tells us that this is a constructor method. A constructor a method that cannot return a value and must be public. It is invoked when an object is instantiated. In this case the method required three parameters, and this is what we supplied to BlueJ. You can think of them as "default settings" for those three parameters. In general, constructors are methods used to setup instances of an object to some known default or initial condition. The only other point to note is the use of the term "this" in the definition of the constructor. We shall consider what "this" means in the next section.

We can also call upon the methods in the Car class. To do this, just right click the object on the workbench and see the public methods that are on offer. The console window will open automatically for the display of messages. You should try that as an exercise and ensure that you understand the logic associated with the design of the Car class. To get the car to move, you need to first start the engine, release the parking brake and press the accelerator. But there is a problem, there is no method to release the parking brake and the default value set by the constructor is ON.

Exercise: Add a new method to the car class to allow the parking brake to be released. You will need it to get the car moving! In Sect. 3.5 we will have a look at a good solution for this exercise.

In this example, the values of the state for car1 and car2 are independent. Although they share the same class design (they are both instances of the Car class), they are distinct objects (they are two separate cars). You will often see a notation like car1: Car meaning car1 is an object of type Car.

At this point, we start to get a sense of what an OO program overall really is. An OO program worthy of the name consists of a set of classes. These classes are then used to create objects and these objects then work together towards some useful collective purpose. You might think at this point that we can't see much evidence of classes working together. After all we have provided just the one Car class definition. But If look closer at the code, we can in fact already see two other Java classes in use that we are working with. We didn't define them, they are part of the broader Java set if library classes. We can identify easily by virtue of the convention that classes start with an upper-case letter. The two classes are String and System. So, what do they do?

The Java String class is used to represent text data. It might not initially seem much of an interesting class because, although it is clearly it has state (the value of the text), it's not obvious that it has methods. After all, what can text "do"? In fact, the Java `String` class has a rich range of methods associated with it. They include such methods as `toUpperCase()` and `toLowerCase()` that converts the text to upper and lower case respectively, and methods that allow you to compare one `String` with another. As `String` is a part of Java, we can use the online documentation from Oracle to get definitive documentation on the `String` class. Here is just an extract:

Method Summary

Methods

Modifier and Type	Method and Description
char	`charAt(int index)` Returns the char value at the specified index.
int	`codePointAt(int index)` Returns the character (Unicode code point) at the specified index.
int	`codePointBefore(int index)` Returns the character (Unicode code point) before the specified index.
int	`codePointCount(int beginIndex, int endIndex)` Returns the number of Unicode code points in the specified text range of this String.
int	`compareTo(String anotherString)` Compares two strings lexicographically.
int	`compareToIgnoreCase(String str)` Compares two strings lexicographically, ignoring case differences.
String	`concat(String str)` Concatenates the specified string to the end of this string.

Source https://docs.oracle.com/javase/7/docs/api/java/lang/String.html

The Oracle documentation is an invaluable tool in programming with Java. It's on-line documentation that allows you to navigate the substantial wealth of classes that are provided for you to use. In fact, whenever we want to solve a programming problem in Java, it is worth checking the documentation to see if one of the many Java classes can do what you need, as it saves you having to write such classes from scratch for yourself. Part of the broader craft of Java programming is having insight and familiarity with the range of existing Java classes.

The `System` class is a somewhat special case in Java. It is the programmatic representation of the Java Virtual Machine (JVM). As Java was designed as a platform independent language, there is no means of communicating directly with the host PC. The very existence of the host is abstracted away from us. The `System` class provides us with a proxy to communicate with the host. As such, there is only ever one host, so it is an example of what we call a "static" or "singleton" class. We don't take any responsibility for creating an instance of the `System` class, there is only instance and, as such, its name is `System`. `System` has a variety of methods including `out.println()` which, as we have seen, causes messages to be printed to the console window.

In both cases, we do not concern ourselves with how `String` or `System` work. That is down to them. All we care about is that we can use them, and that they offer certain state and behaviour characteristics to us. That state and behaviour taken together forms their Application Programming Interface (API) and that is what the Oracle documentation provides us with.

Our car example in fact has three classes working together. As our examples grow more complex, the number of our user defined classes will increase, with due observance of our general OO design principles, and we will make greater and deeper use of the rich set of Java library classes.

3.4   Creating Objects at Run Time

Up to this point we have created an OO program, based on a reasonable OO design, with a single class. That's useful from the perspective of figuring out what a class really is, but the program is still heavily reliant on the user making things happen, like creating the objects and calling the methods. A fuller OO program would have many more classes all working together towards a collective end purpose. It stands to reason that objects need to be able to create and use instances of other objects. In fact, we saw this already when a car object created a `String` object as one of its instance variables (colour in this case).

OO programs need to be able to create new objects as and when they are needed. Unlike other languages (notably C++) we do not need to take any responsibility for getting rid of these objects when they are no longer required. That function (called "garbage collection") is a function of the JVM. Objects are destroyed when the JVM decides that they should be, subject to the rules of scope and the demand for memory.

We shall build on our existing example and build a rather simple car test track. It's simple as it only has space for precisely 3 cars. Not a sophisticated test track, but we will improve our thinking in a later chapter. A test track is a separate entity from a car and thus merits its own class. The test track has a name, can accommodate 3 cars and can be open on closed. When the test track closes, all cars must stop and switch their engines off. That seems a simple enough set of rules, so we define a new class `TestTrack`.

```
/**
 * A simple car test track that can accomodate 3 cars.
 *
 * @author Kingsley Sage
 * @version 1.0
 */
public class TestTrack
{
    // Instance variables ...
    String name;
    Car c1;
    Car c2;
    Car c3;
    boolean isOpen;

    // Constructor method ...

    public TestTrack(String name)
    {
        this.name = name;
        isOpen = true;
        c1 = new Car("red",100, true);
        c2 = new Car("blue", 120, true);
        c3 = new Car("green", 150, false);
    }

    public void runAllCars()
    {
        c1.pressStartButton();
        c2.pressStartButton();
        c3.pressStartButton();
        c1.parkingBrakeOn = false;
        c2.parkingBrakeOn = false;
        c1.pressAccelerator();
        c2.pressAccelerator();
        c3.pressAccelerator(); // What do you think will happen?
    }

    // One other method ...

    public void closeTrack()
    {
        c1.parkingBrakeOn = true;
        c2.parkingBrakeOn = true;
        c3.parkingBrakeOn = true;
        isOpen = false;
        System.out.println("The test track is now closed");
    }
}
```

Once we have added this new `TestTrack` class to our BlueJ project, we have two user defined classes. The BlueJ class panel will now show two orange boxes with a dotted arrow connecting them.

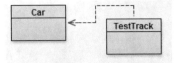

This dotted arrow shows an association or a dependency between the two classes. `TestTrack` relies on `Car` to do its job. This is the start in OO design of a "class diagram". A class diagram shows all the user defined classes and how they relate to one another. We can now right click `TestTrack` to create an instance of it. We then call upon its method `runAllCars()`. The instance of TestTrack appears on the BlueJ workbench:

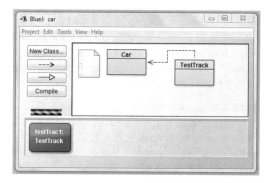

If we inspect our new object we can see that it contains three objects c1, c2 and c3. Note that these 3 objects do not appear on the workbench. This is because we (the user) did not create them. They were created by the object `TestTrac1` which is an object of type `TestTrack (TestTrac1:TestTrack)`. So one object has created three other objects. For the `TestTrac1` object, we see the c1, c2 and c3 objects as arrows in the inspector. You can click on the arrow to drill down into the car objects to see their parameters, as can be seen in the diagram for c1. This shows how useful the BlueJ inspector can be in determining whether the state of an object is what you expect it to be. This is useful when debugging a program when it is not working as expected.

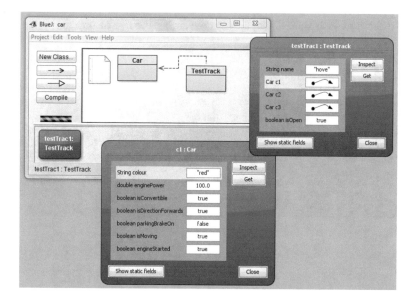

If we run the `runAllCars()` method we get the following output:

```
The red car is moving
The blue car is moving
The parking brake for the green car is on!
```

If you examine the code, it should be apparent why the green car is not moving. We now have a closer look at the `TestTrack` class as it has some elements we have not seen previously. In the `TestTrack` constructor, we see lines of code that look like:

```
c1 = new Car("red",100, true);
c2 = new Car("blue", 120, true);
c3 = new Car("green", 150, false);
```

This is where the three car objects have been created. The keyword `new` is an instruction to the JVM to instantiate a new object of type `Car`. The three parameters are then passed to a matching constructor for action. In this case, a matching constructor would have 3 formal parameters, a `String`, a value that could be a `double` and a `boolean`. We are in luck since this matches the pattern of formal parameters for the only constructor method in our `Car` class. We shall see later that we are able to have multiple constructors to cover different scenarios. In fact, we don't have to have a user defined constructor, it's just a useful thing to do and is good programming craft. If there is no constructor available that matches the signature pattern of parameters (in order and in type), then the Java complier will report an error.

We can now also state a simple rule concerning the use of objects:

An object must be **declared**, and **initialised**.

Declaring an object involves stating what class is it. E.g. `Car c1` declares that "`c1` is a `Car`". But `c1` does not yet exist. The term `c1` is just a label (or "object reference") for an object of that class.

Initialising an object involves creating or "instantiating" an instance of a class. It is usually done using the `new` keyword. E.g. `c1 = new Car();` is the act of initialising the object.

It is possible to declare and initialise an object in one compact line of Java. E.g. `Car c1 = new Car();`

So our three objects c1, c2 and c3 have been initialised. Now we can start to use them. Each of them is of type Car, and has all the state and behaviour associated with the Car class. But TestTrack needs to be specific as to which car object it wishes to refer to. It's no use simply stating pressStartButton() as a method call, as we would not know which of the car objects we were referring to. So we must provide a more fully qualified name. To do that we use the "." notation. This is common in Java and other OO languages. In its simplest form, the notation is:

```
<object reference>.<method/variable name>
```

So c1.pressStartButton() can be read as "call the pressStartButton() method for the object c1". Similarly, c1.parkingBrakeOn = false can be read as "set the parkingBrakeOn instance variable for object c1 to the value false". This notation allows us to be specific about what aspect of state we want to change or method we wish to call for which object.

> **Exercise**: building on the TestTrack example, improve the class so that the track can accommodate 4 cars. Add a method allStop() that causes all cars to come to a stop with their engines off but leaves the track open for business.

We should note here the use of the this keyword we have seen, particularly in constructors. this is a self-referential operator. It is used to mean "this object". In constructors and sometime other methods, we observe that the same variable name is used as a formal parameter in a method call as is used as an instance variable. For example, name in the TestTrack class. If we just refer to some data name, do we mean the formal parameter or the instance variable? The this keyword resolves this ambiguity In this case, this.name refers to the instance variable, and just name refers to the variable of that name most immediately in scope (i.e. the formal parameter in the constructor).

Now our example is getting to the point where we are starting to derive some benefit from using OO. We have two classes, with multiple objects of one of them, and a structure that allows objects to work together to perform some useful task. There is one key element of our OO design principles however that we have not really addressed - encapsulation. All our instance variables (the state data) are currently public. This is because we have not specified that it should be anything else and as such the visibility has defaulted to public. This means that Test-Track can see and modify the state of the car objects. But this is not a sensible model in reality. It is not the role of a test track to apply a parking brake on a car. That's the car's responsibility (in a more sophisticated model, it would be the responsibility of a driver in the car, but we have no class for the driver). We need to improve this part of our thinking. OO is intended to offer a model that is fair an accurate representation of our real-world problem and TestTrack is not really cutting it in this respect. We need to improve our thinking on the encapsulation, and the visibility of state data and methods.

3.5   Accessor and Mutator Methods

We have discussed the concept that all data in a class should be `private` unless there is a useful reason why it should not be. Many programmers argue that the best programming craft is to make ALL data in a class `private`. That way, the only way to interact with objects of that class is through the class API. That is, by calling the methods that are available. This is certainly the model that the Java library classes take. If you look at the on-line documentation for, say, the `String` class, you will see many methods to choose from but no instance variables.

First, let's be clear about how to make data and methods `private` and `public`. To do this you need to add a visibility modifier to the appropriate declaration. If we don't specify a visibility modifier for a variable or a method, the default is `public`. Let's work with a simple two class example involving books:

```java
/**
 * A simple Book class
 *
 * @author Kingsley Sage
 * @version 1.0
 */
public class Book
{
    // Instance variables (all made public) ...
    public String title;
    public String author;
    public double value;

    // Constructor
    public Book (String title, String author, double value)
    {
        this.title = title;
        this.author = author;
        this.value = value;
    }
}


/**
 * A class to represent a small shelf used for books
 *
 * @author Kingsley Sage
 * @version 1.0
 */
public class Shelf
{
    public Book b1;
    public Book b2;

    // Constructor
    public Shelf()
    {
        b1 = new Book("100 Lobster Recipes","Dan Smith",10.50);
        b2 = new Book("70s Rock Music","Rick Flash",20.0);
    }

    public void changeValues()
    {
        b1.value = 9.50;
        b1.value = 18.00;
    }
}
```

So we can create an instance of the `Shelf` class and call the `changeValues()` method if we like and it will work fine. This is because the value variable in the `Book` class is `public`. This means that an object outside of `Book` can have access to that `value` variable and do anything it likes with it, including change its value. The code is simple, but there are no restrictions on what external objects may subsequently change the value of the `value` variable, and that has the potential to undermine the integrity of the codebase. Really it up the `Book` class to look after its own information. So we make a subtle change to the `Book` class:

```
/**
 * A simple Book class
 *
 * @author Kingsley Sage
 * @version 1.0
 */

public class Book
{
    // Instance variables (all made private) ...
    private String title;
    private String author;
    private double value;

    // Constructor
    public Book (String title, String author, double value)
    {
        this.title = title;
        this.author = author;
        this.value = value;
    }
}
```

This time the instance variables have been made `private`. This means that they can only be accessed from within the `Book` class e.g. inside the constructor or other methods specifically defined within the scope of the `Book` class. This helps us achieve the desired encapsulation characteristic but gives us a problem. The `changeValues()` method in the `Shelf` class is no longer able to access the `value` attribute in the `Book` class, as it is `private` to the `Book` class. As such, the complier will complain that the `Shelf` class has no visibility of the `value` attribute in the `Book` class. So what if another class really does have a purpose in accessing or changing some of the state data inside the `Book` objects?

Achieving this is the role of two special sets of methods; accessors and mutators.

In reality, there is nothing special about the definitions of accessor and mutator methods. There are no special Java keywords to characterise them. They are just a set of methods written to a set of conventions. But as a concept they have clear definitions:

An **accessor** method returns the value of a private piece of data within an instance of a class. By convention, an accessor starts with the word `get` followed by the variable name that it refers to. For example, `getX()` is a method that returns the value of a variable x.

A **mutator** method allows the value of a private piece of data within an instance of a class to be altered. By convention, a mutator starts with the word `set` followed by the variable that it refers to. For example, `setX(<parameter>)` is a method that allows the value of variable x to be altered.

So now we add an example accessor and mutator method to the `Book` class:

```
public double getValue()
{
    return value;
}

public void setValue(double newValue)
{
    value = newValue;
}
```

Note the naming conventions—they are not enforced by the compiler, they are just good code craft and other programmers would recognise them immediately. Following these naming conventions saves you having to think of what the names would be for any accessor or mutator. Now our `Shelf` object can use the `setValue()` mutator method to change the value of the books:

```
public void changeValues()
{
    b1.setValue(9.50);
    b2.setValue(18.00);
}
```

In essence, the `Shelf` class has to "ask" the `Book` class to change its own value. Responsibility for changing the value variable for a book object rests with the book object and that is where is truly belongs. You may think at first glance this seems a lot of code for no real practical benefit other than making us feel better in our OO design principles. But there is a very real reason why this is a good idea. Now that the responsibility for altering the value variable is built as a method, that method can use whatever code required to enforce validity constraints on the values that the variable can take on. For, example, we can prevent another object from setting a negative value. We just make the mutator a bit more sophisticated:

```
public void setValue(double newValue)
{
    if (newValue > 0.0)
    {
        value = newValue;
    }
    else
    {
        System.out.println("Not acceptable value");
        // And the old value remains ...
    }
}
```

The visibility modifiers also apply to methods as well. If a method is declared as `public`, then it can be called by an object outside of that class. Accessor and mutator methods therefore by definition should be `public`. If we declare a method to be `private` then it can only be called within that class. This may seem initially rather useless, but remember that a more complex class may have a large number of methods. Only some of them are intended for external usage (i.e. they form part of the API for that class). Others are just part of the inner workings of that class and are there to assist in a structured and orderly implementation of that class.

This approach helps us to build more robust programs. This is important in an age where we come to rely on software systems. If we can make a program operate with invalid data either through carelessness in further design and coding, or through malicious exploits, then the actions of that program become hard to determine. The consequences can vary from irritating to critical e.g. where systems form part of a control system in aerospace applications. By using accessors and mutators, we can exercise fine grained control over state data. If we make the `Book` value `private` and then only provide an accessor method, then the value can never be changed accidentally. The value then becomes a "read only" attribute. If we decide that the value can be changed, then we can dictate how it can be changed. So the use of accessors and mutators not only supports our OO encapsulation principle, it helps us build better and more reliable software.

3.6   Choosing the Right Classes

Now that we understand the basic concepts of what OO design and coding is all about, it's worth reflecting on some general principles for choosing the right classes. If we choose wisely, coding should follow easily. The examples in this capture have been necessarily simple. We will develop our understanding further as we progress through the subsequent chapters. But there are some useful guidelines that we can develop now that will help us. We have discussed that a good class is highly cohesive—it focusses on representing one entity and does it well. Where we have multiple classes, each class should have a distinct, cohesive and clearly defined purpose. In the cars example, the `Car` class represented a single car.

The `TestTrack` represented a place where cars could be driven (physically a different thing). We can characterise this relationship as a "has-a". That is, a `TestTrack` "has" cars. It also has its own unique attributes as well, hence they are different classes. In general, where this "has-a" or "uses" relationship exists, it suggests in OO design terms that we are dealing with properly distinct classes. But sometimes the relationship is different. Some classes have a hierarchal relationship with each other. One possible example here would be a Gift class for use in an online shopping application. A shop sells many Gifts and a `Gift` is clearly a good candidate for a class. But there are many different types of Gift. The notion of a `Gift` could be further refined into a `Book`, a `Game` or an `Ornament`. These are also reasonable classes in their own right. But there is an "is-a" relationship between these classes. An `Ornament` is an entity but also "is-a" gift. That suggest a different kind of relationship (called a super and sub class) and we shall explore that in Chap. 5.

Say we wanted to collect cars. We decide that we need a class that represents our collection of cars. Maybe we decide to call it `MyCollectionOfCars` and populate it with some instances of car objects. However, the collection isn't really a new class, it's just one or more instances of the `Car` class, with little other data to add. In this case, what we really want is a Java collection of type `Car`, and that does not require us to produce a new class, but instead to draw on Java library classes that deal with collections, and we explore this in the next chapter.

Library Classes and Packages

4

In this chapter, we delve into some of the rich pre-built code libraries that make Java a useful language for a wide range of applications. In truth, the libraries that exist as at version 8 of the language are so rich and varied that it is unlikely that many programmers, even experienced professionals, have an encyclopaedic knowledge of them all. New libraries are developed all the time with many new ones appearing in open source repositories. Part of the skill of being a good programmer isn't knowing what all he libraries are, rather having a feel of what should exist, and having the ability to use documentation to figure out how to extract the maximum value from them. As a general principle, whenever we want to solve some problem, like sorting data, using network connections, creating a GUI, playing sound and much more, it is always worth spending some time investigating whether a Java library already exists that offers what you need. As long as you are sure of the credentials of the library (particularly in respect of open source content) and you are aware of any licensing conditions that apply in the deployment of a library (important if you plan to sell your coding skills or create a commercial application) then you will be fine.

4.1 Organisation of Java into the Core and Packages

The Java language forms part of a broader Java ecosystem. As well as the language itself, there are tools, applications and frameworks that enable you to build a vast range of applications from desktop to mobile, web applets and large-scale distributed enterprise systems using the EE 8 Jakarta framework. But at the heart of this ecosystem is the Java language, currently in version 11. The language has developed a great deal since its first inception in 1995. The language consists of core functionality and an extended landscape consisting of packages containing library classes. The class library provides well over 3000 classes for programmers to use.

© Springer Nature Switzerland AG 2019
K. Sage, *Concise Guide to Object-Oriented Programming*,
Undergraduate Topics in Computer Science,
https://doi.org/10.1007/978-3-030-13304-7_4

The core of the language incorporates all the basic syntactic structures required to afford sequence, alternation and repetition and a range of frequently used classes such as `String` (used to manage pieces of text), the `System` proxy object (to facilitate communication with the JVM) and others. No specific coding measures are needed to utilise the core of the language, other than to correctly adhere to the syntax of the language.

In common with other languages such as C/C++, the core of the language can be augmented by functionality drawn from libraries (C programmers will be familiar with the use of the `#include` directive to do exactly that). These additional classes are organised into thematic groups, or packages. A package might contain just a few additional classes, or several tens of them. For example, there are packages for managing HTTP requests, or working with SQL databases. Each of these packages consists of pre-built Java byte code that can be utilised directly, provided that the programmer understands the Application Programming Interface (API) that it provides.

4.2 Using Library Classes

To use a library class turns out to be very simple. The byte code resides in a directory within the JDK/JRE. To access it you simply use the `import` directive. This directive tells the JVM that the library byte code will be used in a current project. You can opt to import just a single class, but it is often easier simply to import an entire package. To import an entire package you simply replace the name of the specific class with the wildcard * character. This is no particular disbenefit from importing the entire package. The necessary `import` directives are placed at the top of any class that needs to use them. The directives are outside the class definition itself:

```
import java.util.Random;
// imports the Random class from the java.util package

import java.util.*;
// imports all classes from the java.util package.
```

The `import` directive is simply syntactic sugar intended to prevent name space clashes. All Java classes are members of a package somewhere in the Java landscape. For example, `String` is actually a member of the `java.lang` package. But that package is imported by default by the Java compiler. The notion of packages gives rise to the concept of a "fully qualified name". For example, the `String` class is more fully known as `java.lang.String`, but that's inconvenient for such a frequently used class. In fact, all library classes can be used at any time simply be referring to them by their fully qualified names. But that isn't convenient and makes the code we write less clear. So we use the packages and generally just import what we need.

You can also build your code into your own packages, and then re-use that package at a later stage in another project. This promotes the highly desirable concept of code re-use, and many professional programmers build their own packages and libraries over time to speed up projects where pre-built code can be re-used.

The on-line Oracle documentation always specifies which package a class belongs to. That information can be found at the top of the page for that class. For example, if we look at the documentation for the `String` class:

Source https://docs.oracle.com/javase/9/docs/api/java/lang/String.html

we learn that `String` is indeed from the `java.lang` package. We already saw some examples of the `import` directive in the guessing game program in Chap. 2.

4.3 The `String` Class

The `String` class is probably the most widely used class in the Java language. It is used to store and manipulate text. In some languages, notably C, such text has to be stored and manipulated as an array of primitive characters. Whilst that is conceptually sound, it's not convenient, and Java does rather better in this respect. We firsts saw the `String` class in Chap. 3, but it's worth spending more time now getting to understand some of the finer details.

As a class, an object of type `String` has fields (attributes) and methods. In fact, the `String` class only has one attribute and is not often used. Instead, all the work on `String` objects is done using methods. This is a common Java coding philosophy: *"If something needs to be done, there should be a public method to do it"*. As we saw in Chap. 3, that extends to setting and retrieving objects values using accessor and mutator methods.

All string literals ("pieces of text") in Java are implemented as instances of the `String` class. In fact `String` objects are constant or "immutable". This means that once they have been set, their text content (their value) cannot be altered. There is an alternative to `String` that allows the text content to be edited—the

StringBuffer class. If you need to change the value of a String object, you simply overwrite the old text content with the new.

Of note to C enthusiasts, a String is implemented at a lower-level as a fixed length array of type char. As instances of a class, we recall that String objects need to be declared and initialised. However, as they are so frequently used, some syntactic shortcuts have been added to the language to enable you to do that quickly and easily. Here are some examples of how to declare and initialise String objects:

```
// Separate declaration and initialisation
String s1;
s1 = new String("Skywalker");

// Combined declaration and initialisation
String s2 = new String("Leia");

// Combined and shortened syntax form
String s3 = "Vader";
```

The name of the String object as declared forms what is termed an "object reference". It is somewhat similar in concept to the notion of a pointer in the C language, but it is not as low-level, as Java does not support direct access to the host PC other than via the System object. In fact this is true for all objects, not just those of type String. An object reference is used to refer to an object by name, for example, when we wish to pass an object to a method. An object reference can exist independently of an actual object. It is also the case that an actual object in memory can have more than one reference to it. The following code example will help you understand this:

```
String s1 = "Yoda";
String s2 = "Dent";
String s3;

System.out.println(s1); // produces "Yoda"
System.out.println(s2); // produces "Dent"

s3 = s2;
System.out.println(s3); // produces "Dent"

s3 = s1;
System.out.println(s3); // produces "Yoda"

s1 = "Ewok";
System.out.println(s3); // produces "Yoda"
```

In this example, s1, s2 and s3 are all objects references for an object of type String. The content of s1 and s2 are initialised, but s3 is just an object reference with no object initially for it to refer to (it has a default value of null meaning "no object"). But then s3 is set equal to s2. This does not create a new object for s3, it just makes s3 a temporary pseudonym for s2. So when we display s3, we actually see the text content for s2. We can change the object that s3 refers to as often as we want. When we set s3 = s1 and display s3 we get the expected text content "Yoda". We then change s1 to "Ewok". But what happens now is that s1 now refers to a new object (remember that the String class is immutable, so its value has been replaced with a new object). So s1 has its new text content, but what about s3? The text content that s3 refers to still exists, but s1 no longer refers to it, but s3 does. So s3 is no longer a pseudonym for s1, they now refer to distinct objects in memory in their own right.

It is important to note that if you want to compare two String objects, you need to take care to understand whether it's the objects (as they exist in memory within the JVM) or the text content of the objects that you want to compare. If we apply the test s1 == s2, we are asking if object references s1 and s2 refer to the same object. They may well do, in which case the text content would be the same, but they may also be two distinct objects in memory that may, or may not, have the same text content. If we wish to test whether two String objects have the same text content, there are methods specifically for that (namely compareTo() and compareToIgnoreCase()—see the examples below).

The String class has a range of methods available to it. They allow you to do a range of useful things including:

- Establish how many characters there are in the text content.
- Change the case form upper to lower and vice versa.
- Compare the text content of one String to the text content of another.
- Extract a sub-section, or sub string of the text content.

Here are some examples of some of the key String methods in use:

```java
public void stringExamples()
{
    String s1 = "Woodpecker";
    String s2 = "Starling";
    String s3 = "  starling";

    // length() tells us how many characters are
    // in the text content of a String

    System.out.println("s1 has " + s1.length() + " chars");

    // charAt() is a method that picks a single
    // character out of a String
```

```
    for (int x=0; x < s1.length(); x++)
    {
        System.out.println(s1.charAt(x));
    }

    // trim() eliminates whitespace around a String
    // Note that we replace s3 with its new value
    // as String objects are immutable

    s3 = s3.trim();

    // compareTo() compares the text content of two Strings
    // The method produces a value of 0 only if the two strings
    // have identical content including matching case

    int y;
    y = s2.compareTo(s3);
    System.out.println(y);

    // compareToIgnoreCase() does something similar,
    // but is case insensitive, so here we expect the
    // returned value to be 0

    int z;
    z = s2.compareToIgnoreCase(s3);
    System.out.println(z);
}
```

Note that for the charAt() method, the characters are referred to using a "zero indexed" numbering system. That is, the first character element in a String is located at position 0. So a String with 5 characters has 5 characters elements in positions number 0 to 4 inclusively. This zero indexing strategy is widely used throughout Java and is commonplace in most other programming languages.

For a full account of the String methods, visit the Oracle on-line documentation. It's easy to find, using any decent search engine use a search term like "Java String" and the official class page will likely be the very first result. Each page provides details of all the publicly available functionality of that class. The documentation constitutes the Application Programming Interface (API) for that class.

4.4 Application Programming Interfaces (APIs)

The broad field of software engineering has made considerable advances over the decades since the first programming languages of the 1950s. When the earliest languages such as COBOL and FORTRAN first emerged, they were the domain of a small number of specialists who truly understood how to leverage their features to solve practical problems. In more modern times, we have a wealth of fully featured languages that are widely accessible to a global community of developers. Part of this is down to the widespread availability of computing devices, and part is down to the fact that we can rely on elements of software that others have already built as building blocks for new applications. Very few problems require completely unique solutions. The concept of software re-use has become a central theme in modern software engineering. This has led to improvements in reliability, reduced costs and shorter development times. The open source community leads the way in distributed code development and incremental improvements (just consider the way that an open source project such as the Linux operating system is continually evolving).

A core concept in achieving the goal of effective software re-use is the idea of an Application Programming Interface (API). The idea is a natural extension of the concept of a method. We create methods with a characteristic signature of a set of formal parameters and a return value. We can invoke the method and rely on the fact that it does the job it was created to do. We do not have to concern ourselves with how the method works unless we choose to. All any calling code or coder needs to know is how to use it, and what it does and not how it does it. We say that we have "abstracted away" the internal implementation details.

This is very much how we should view an OO language such as Java. The extended Java landscape provides over 3000 classes. We use them by simply understanding via appropriate documentation as to what they do and how to use them. We do not concern ourselves with implementation details. In fact the separation of the API from its underlying implementation can allow programs written in one language to use a library written in another. A good example is Java and Scala. Both of these languages compile to compatible byte code. Code written in Scala can offer a Java like API and be called by Java code. The calling Java code is agnostic of the fact that the underlying implementation is in fact in another language. So a single API can be used across multiple implementations in different languages.

These ideas place a strong emphasis on understanding what something does and this, in turn, demands a meaningful scheme to document it. The value of an API is determined by how well it is documented so that we can understand how to use it. The API should describe what the behaviour of the library should be under all situations. The API should only make public those features that are intended for use by the calling code. The underlying implementation may have many elements and parts to it, but these should be abstracted away and fall under the auspices of the implementation. All of this provides us with some general software engineering principles that we should adhere to when we create any significant code:

1. Any single class should be designed to represent one entity, and do that job well (principle of cohesion).
2. Classes should only make public those attributes and methods that are intended for use by calling code. All other attributes and methods should remain private (principle of encapsulation).
3. Consideration should be given to grouping classes together in thematic packages.
4. Where practical, classes should share common interfaces and interface patterns (the concept of design patterns).

5. Classes should be adequately documented such that they can be used by other programmers (and potentially in other coding environments) without any knowledge of their internal implementation.
6. Class documentation should be kept up to date with incremental improvements in the class codebase. Out of date software documentation is a major impediment to effective re-use.
7. Classes should be robust against incorrect data being fed to them, and should respond in an appropriate manner by reporting errors, and raising appropriate error conditions to prevent poor data affecting other parts of a software system.

The concept of classes sharing common interfaces will be discussed further in Chap. 5 where we explore abstract classes and interfaces.

Dealing with errors is a complex subject in its own right. Java has some sophisticated means of responding to error condition using the concept of exception handling and we explore this further in Chap. 6.

The on-line Oracle documentation provides an excellent example of what class level APIs should look like. Each class is described in terms of its package membership, the `public` fields and methods and the formal and returned parameters for each method, combined with textual descriptions of the class and its attributes and methods, with worked examples of how to use them in practice. Creating such documentation may seem a daunting prospect, particularly in respect of keeping it up to date as software evolves. Before the development of appropriate tools to assist in maintaining documentation, it would have been a full-time role in a professional software team. But in reality the best place to keep software documentation is within the software itself.

In the next section we learn how to create this standard of documentation for classes that we create.

4.5   Using Javadocs in BlueJ

Javadocs is a software documentation tool and is part of the Java Development Toolkit. It is a standalone application that automatically produces class level API documentation for our code. This is significant as in the previous section we discussed that the best place to keep software documentation is within the software itself. But Java on its own cannot produce the documentation for us. To create the documentation, we need to "markup" or annotate the codebase in a particular manner so that the Javadocs tool can do its job and create the API documentation.

There are two types of markup that we need to consider:

- **Commenting**: by laying out multi-line code comments in a particular manner, we can provide information about what a class does, and what methods in that class do.
- **Annotations**: using particular non-code annotations to indicate the purpose of some aspect of the codebase. In Java, annotations are demoted using the @ symbol. The annotations and comments are ignored by the complier—they are there solely to serve our documentation needs.

Once we have marked up the code appropriately, the Javadocs tool can be used to extract the markup data from the code and produce our API documentation. Whilst the Javadocs tool can be manually invoked, BlueJ offers us a convenient way in the code editor to switch between a source code view and a documentation view. If you look at the top right corner of the BlueJ code editor, you will see a drag down control with options for "Source Code" or "Documentation". Whenever you switch to documentation view mode, the Javadocs tool is invoked and parses the markup data in the class file and produces a HTML compliant file with the API documentation in it. This documentation is then stored in folder within the project directory. The HTML documentation can then be distributed as the API documentation and viewed on any browser.

Let's look an example of a very simple class designed to perform some mathematical operations. The class is not very advanced in its implementation yet:

```
/**
 * A class that performs some simple maths operations.
 *
 * @author Kingsley Sage
 * @version 1.0
 */
public class SimpleMaths
{
    /**
     * Constructor: to be developed further
     */
    public SimpleMaths()
    {
    }

    /**
     * Returns the sum of two integers.
     * @param x: an integer
     * @param y: an integer
     * @return the integer sum of x and y
     */
    public int addTwoNumbers(int x, int y)
    {
        return x+y;
    }
}
```

We see that the class `SimpleMaths` currently has one constructor method and one other method `addTwoNumbers()`. The multiline comments have been started with `/**` and ended with `**/`. This signifies to Javadocs that these comments form part of the markup. The class as a whole has a description and it is further annotated with `@author` and `@version`, both of which are self-explanatory. Both the methods have similar basic annotations, but `addTwoNumbers()` is further marked up with `@param` and `@return` annotations. Each `@param` marks up one of the formal parameters, and `@return` marks up the returned parameter.

If we now switch the BlueJ editor to documentation view, we see:

We see that our markup has been used to produce Oracle style API documentation, complete with hyperlink navigation.

All we now need to do is to ensure that as we incrementally update the codebase, that we keep our commenting and annotations up to date, and we will always have the means to produce the API documentation on demand. There are other annotations as well, and we shall see some of them in later chapters.

We should consider what further documentation may be required beyond the Javadocs standard. Although the purpose of API documentation is to provide other with sufficient knowledge to use a class, that does not mean that further commenting is not appropriate. Other developers may be required to refine the implementation later. To that end, we should comment to a level that would enable another developer to make sense of what we have done. Failure to comment and document code properly can mean that it is cheaper to abandon existing codebases and start again from scratch when you want to innovate.

Although attributes and methods that are `private` do not form part of the API documentation, it is worth documenting them to the same standard as part of a broader effort to ensure that the software is as reusable and maintainable as possible, and such practices should be regarded as the norm in professional software engineering.

4.6 The **ArrayList** Class

We have seen that data can be stored in primitive types and in the form of objects. But up to now each piece of data has corresponded to one example of data of that type. An object represents one instance of a class—one example of an entity. One of the driving reasons for building programs in an OO manner is to allow us to model better some real-world problem.

One key aspect of a problem that we will want to model is "collections of things". For example, if we were building a football video game, we might decide that a player was an appropriate entity to model and thus a good choice for a class. But players also work together to make a team—a collection of players. In the same way, a word processor document is just a collection of paragraphs. A paragraph is a collection of sentences and a sentence is a collection of words. So the concept of a collection is commonplace in the real world, and thus it makes sense for Java to offer us a way of representing one.

Java has many possible means of representing collections. Probably the most commonly used is the ArrayList class (part of the java.util package). This class is very flexible and is designed to address several collection related requirements:

- It can be used to store a collection of any Java class type. We say that the ArrayList class is a generic one. However, it cannot be used directly to create collections of primitive types. We discuss a solution for this in the next section.
- The collection must consist of elements of the same type. So we may have a collection of String, Bicycle or whatever, but they must all be of the same type. It is possible to have collections of seemingly mixed types as long as they share a common super type. We will explore this idea in Chap. 5.
- The collection can be of arbitrary size, subject to any memory limitations of the JVM and the host machine.
- At any time we can determine how many elements are in the collection
- We can perform a range of collection related operations such as adding new objects to the collection, removing an object, clearing all objects, and retrieving and object from the collection.
- The collection is a Java object in its own right. It is an object that incorporates a collection of other objects.
- There are a range of algorithms designed to work with generic classes to perform commonplace operations such as sorting. This is discussed further in Chap. 7.

In order to use the ArrayList, we need to:

- Import the java.util package for any class that will use the ArrayList.
- Declare and initialise the ArrayList.

- Use the `ArrayList` API to determine how to use the methods offered by the class.

The only significant new syntax we need to master relates to the generic nature of `ArrayList`. This generic nature is not confined to the `ArrayList`. The general form of the declaration and initialisation of the `ArrayList` is as follows:

```
import java.util.*;

<access-modifier> ArrayList< <object-type> > <field-name>

<field-name> = new ArrayList< <object-type> > ();
```

Note that the object type appears after the keyword `ArrayList` in angular brackets e.g. `ArrayList<String>` is an `ArrayList` of type `String`.

As an example, we build a simple `Dictionary` class. A dictionary is simply a collection of words. We can represent a word conveniently as a `String`, so our `Dictionary` will require a collection of `String`. Our dictionary will then incorporate some additional functionality, so allow us to add words, and to check whether words are present (i.e. the start of a design of a simple spell checker).

Here is the start of our `Dictionary` class:

```
import java.util.*;

/**
 * A simple dictionary to illustrate the ArrayList in use.
 *
 * @author Kingsley Sage
 * @version 1.0
 */
public class Dictionary
{
    // Instance variables
    private ArrayList<String> words;

    /**
     * Constructor for Dictionary
     */
    public Dictionary()
    {
        // Initialise the ArrayList
        words = new ArrayList<String>();
        addInitialWords();
    }

    // Further methods to be added here …
}
```

The addInitialWords() method will be defined shortly. First, we consider what some of the key methods are available from the ArrayList API:

Method	Description
boolean add(E e)	Add an element e of type E to the end of the collection
void clear()	Remover all elements from the collection
E get(int index)	Retrieve element of type E from position index
boolean isEmpty()	Returns true if the collection is empty
E remove(int index)	Removes the element from position index of the collection (returns that element of type E)
int size()	Returns the number of elements in the collection
boolean contains (Object o)	Returns true if the list contains the specified element o

We start by adding a method to put some words in our Dictionary:

```
/**
 * Adds some initial words to the words ArrayList.
 * @param none
 * @return none
 */
public void addInitialWords()
{
    words.add("crocodile");
    words.add("antelope");
    words.add("gnu");
    words.add("zebra");
    words.add("giraffe");
}
```

Note that "crocodile" here is just a syntactic shorthand for new String("crocodile").

These String objects now form the elements of the collection. So the words field now has a total of 5 elements. Following the zero-indexing concept we saw for the String class, the elements are numbers as members of the collection at index 0 through to N-1 where N is the size() of the collection. Management of the memory within the JVM for the storage of the elements is automatic—the ArrayList will expand and shrink in memory terms as we use it.

We could now add a simple method to display all the words currently in the Dictionary. This can be done conveniently using a for loop:

```
/**
 * Display all words in the ArrayList
 * @param none
 * @return none
 */
public void displayAllWords()
{
    for (int i=0; i < words.size(); i++)
    {
        // Retrieve the String at position i
        String w = words.get(i);
        System.out.println(w);
    }
}
```

Using a loop in this way is referred to as "iterating through the collection". At this point it is worth considering an alternative syntactic construction for iterating through an `ArrayList` using a variant of the `for` loop (often referred to as a for each loop):

```
/**
 * Display all words in the ArrayList using for each
 * @param none
 * @return none
 */
public void displayAllWords2()
{
    for (String w:words)
    {
        System.out.println(w);
    }
}
```

In this case, we read `String w:words` as "for each `String w` in `words`". The variable `w` of type `String` becomes the iteration variable and the loop linearly iterates through the loop one element at a time making the value of `w` the next element in the `ArrayList`.

Finally we add two other useful methods:

- `checkWord()`: to allow us to determine whether a word is present or not.
- `addNewWord()`: so that we can add new words to our `Dictionary` (provided the word is unique).

```
/**
 * Add a new word to the ArrayList
 * @param word as a String
 * @return true if the word added is unique, false otherwise
 */
public boolean addNewWord(String w)
{
    if (checkWord(w) == false)
    {
        words.add(w);
        return true;
    }
    else
    {
        return false;
    }
}

/**
 * check to see whether a word is in the dictionary
 * @param word as a String
 * @return true if the word is present in the dictionary
 */
public boolean checkWord(String w)
{
    boolean x;
    x = words.contains(w);
    if (x == true)
    {
        // w is already in the dictionary
        return false;
    }
    else
    {
        return true;
    }
}
```

So we have the start of a useful Dictionary class. With a little more effort, we could expand it so that we could enter a whole sentence (as a String), break that sentence down into individual words (an ArrayList of String) and then check each word. The dictionary is not yet very efficient, as the words are not arranged in any particular order (other than the order in which they were added to the list), and this would not scale well. But we will return to this example in Chap. 7 when we look at other collection types and some of the algorithms available for use with generic classes such as ArrayList.

4.7 The Wrapper Classes

We have seen that `ArrayList` can be used to create a collection of any Java object. But Java also features a set of primitive non-object types such as `int`. It is desirable to have the ability to form collections of these on a similar basis to any other object. But the status of the primitive types is not conducive to the generic object nature of the `ArrayList`. Rather than dilute the concept of the `Array-List` and have a completely separate collection just for the primitives, Java offers a neat solution in the form of a set of classes that allow the primitive types to be packaged in a manner that allows them to function as objects, specifically for the purpose of interacting with other Java classes that require object status for their operation. We call these the wrapper classes.

A wrapper class essentially provides an object construction in memory that embeds the primitive type (that provides the underlying attribute for an object of that class), and provides appropriate methods to permit that attribute to be initialised and read i.e. constructor and accessor methods. The wrapper classes also provide a surprising range of other methods designed to, among other things, convert `String` representations of numeric data into numeric data (e.g. the `String` "123" into the `int 123`) and to convert numeric types between different memory size representations (e.g. `int` to `long`, `long` to `double` and so on). But most of the time, we use the wrapper classes to perform their most core job of allowing primitive types to act as objects. Each of the primitive types has a corresponding wrapper class including:

Primitive type	Wrapper class
byte	Byte
int	Integer
long	Long
short	Short
double	Double

If we use the `Integer` wrapper class an example, we can examine the class API and we find some key constructors and methods:

Constructor	Description
Integer(int value)	Creates an object that represents the specified `int` value
Integer(String s)	Creates an object that represents the `int` value specific by the `String s`
Key methods	
int intValue()	Returns the underlying value as an `int`
double doubleValue()	Returns the underlying value after conversion of the primitive `int` to `double`

To create an instance of a wrapped `int`, we use the constructors:

```
public class WrapperTest
{
    Integer x1, x2;

    public WrapperTest()
    {
        x1 = new Integer(10);
        x2 = new Integer("123");
    }
}
```

If we need to access the values as primitives, we use the accessor method `intValue()`:

```
    public void accessValues()
    {
        int y1 = x1.intValue();
        int y2 = x2.intValue();
        int y3 = y1 + y2;
        System.out.println("y3 = " + y3);
    }
```

If we want to update the `int` value, just overwrite the original `Integer` object, as the wrapper objects themselves are immutable (the same as the `String` class), so here we could just use `y2 = new Integer(y3)` and that will use the primitive `y3` value above and re-wrapper it in the object `x2`, displacing the original object that `x2` referred to.

Now we can use any of the suitably wrapped primitive types with other library classes such as `ArrayList`. Here is an example of a program that can generate an `ArrayList` of random numbers of any size as specified by the user in the constructor:

```java
import java.util.*;

/**
 * Creates an ArrayList of random numbers in the
 * range 1-99 inclusively.
 *
 * @author Kingsley Sage
 * @version 1.0
 */

public class ListGenerator
{
    private ArrayList<Integer> myList;

    /**
     * Constructor
     * @param num number of initial elements in the list
     */
    public ListGenerator(int num)
    {
        Random r = new Random();
        myList = new ArrayList<Integer>();
        for (int i=0; i<num; i++)
        {
            int x = r.nextInt(99)+1;
            myList.add(new Integer(x));
        }
    }

    /**
     * Displays each number in the list on the console
     * @param none
     * @return none
     */
    public void displayList()
    {
        for (Integer i:myList)
        {
            System.out.println(i.intValue());
        }
    }
}
```

Now that we understand the basic concepts of classes and the extended landscape of the Java language, we can start to deepen our understanding of the OO paradigm and really start to exploit the nature of an entity and our ability to capture and model it effectively in code. To do that we must turn our attention to one of the most core features of OO languages—polymorphism.

Modelling the World the Object Oriented Way

5

As we have previously discussed, one of the reasons we build OO programs is because they allow us to produce code that provides a useful model of some real-world problem, using classes to represent entities in our problem domain. Up to now, each class has represented a disjoint entity, each with a clear and distinct purpose. But the real world is more complex than that. In this chapter we explore how we can use a deeper understanding of OO principles to produce programs with a structure that is better suited to a real-world problem. Understanding the content of this chapter is key to making the most out of an OO language such as Java.

5.1 Hierarchies in the Real World

As societies, we have a tendency to organise and function using hierarchical structures. For example, the staffing structures in traditional human resource management, with a CEO at the top of the structure, deputies and senior managers beneath that, followed by team leaders and workers. Such structures are useful in making the day to day operations of an organisation manageable. In a retail shop, products are organised and managed in thematic grouping such as hard goods, perishable foods and so on. Such groupings form an integral part of the stock control and checkout management operations. We often use tree diagrams and organograms to capture and visualise these relationships. For example, for the retail shop example:

© Springer Nature Switzerland AG 2019
K. Sage, *Concise Guide to Object-Oriented Programming*,
Undergraduate Topics in Computer Science,
https://doi.org/10.1007/978-3-030-13304-7_5

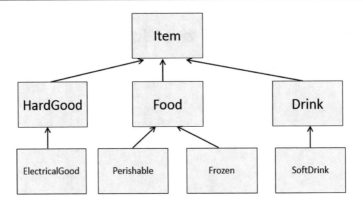

In the context of OO design, we are interested in hierarchies that represent the progressive design of a set of classes. The root of our design is a relatively abstract entity, and we build upon that entity to produce progressively more concrete entities. Considering our previous example closer up:

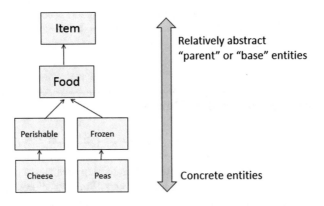

We note that the entity of an Item is relatively abstract in the sense that we could not go into a shop and purchase one. If we said to a member of staff that we "wish to purchase an item", we would expect the response "which item?". We can purchase specific, or concrete entities, but not those that are relatively abstract in their conceptualisation. But that does not mean that the higher-level entities have no value. They just serve as base definitions onto which we can build more concrete entities. We say that that the higher-level entities are "parent", "base" or "super" classes, and the lower-level ones built from them are "child" or "sub" classes.

The key idea here is the "is-a" relationship. Looking at our shop example, we see that HardGood is-a Item and that ElectricalGood is-a HardGood and by extension is-a Item. That suggests that, in type terms, ElectricalGood has type ElectricalGood and also has type of HardGood and ultimately Item. This is the kind of hierarchical relationship that Java and other OO programs are designed to capture.

Not every real-world hierarchy as we might construe it is suited to this kind of super and sub class analysis. Consider the human resources example referred to earlier. The CEO is the head of the organisation, but does not make much sense as a base class. A senior manager is not also the CEO. A team member is not also a senior manager. So instead of the classic staffing organogram that you might be used to seeing, a more appropriate OO relationship might look something like this:

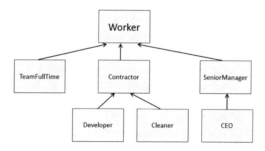

Such an OO compatible hierarchical relationship is an example of the key OO concept of "polymorphism".

Polymorphism at the class level is the concept that an object can take on more than one form. If an object of class type X has a parent class of type Y, then X can take the form of an object of type either X or Y, and can thus appear in many forms.

As we shall see later in Sect. 5.4, polymorphism is not confined to the class level. But for now, we shall develop our notions of class level polymorphism in terms of what it means in Java coding.

5.2   Introducing Super and Sub-classes

Class level polymorphism in Java is implemented using the idea of super and classes. In OO design terms we need to consider what attributes and methods a set of classes share. Where we can identify common attributes and methods, we can factorise the design of those classes so that the commonly shared attributes and methods form part of the super class. We will use an example to help us understand how this works. Consider a shop that sells antiques items, namely vases, statues and paintings. For now we shall consider just some appropriate attributes for our initial OO analysis:

Vase
value
height
material
creator

Statue
value
weight
creator
colour

Painting
value
height
width
isWatercolour
isFramed
creator

We will make three classes for each of the things that our shop sells. We can see that the classes have some attributes in common, and some that are unique to each class. But we can also see that in reality all three classes are examples of "items"—things that the shop sells. So we can factorise our design with an Item superclass, and then make our three specific classes a sub class of that super class. This is beneficial as it reduces un-necessary code duplication (as well as being a better model of a real-world problem).

The super and sub class relationship is represented by an arrow pointing from the sub class towards its super class:

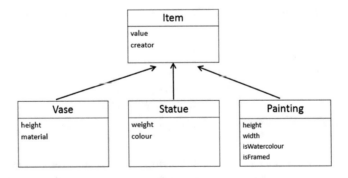

We can now create some classes in Java to represent the super class Item and the three sub classes Vase, Statue and Painting. The keyword extends is used to indicate in Java that a class is a sub class of another:

```
/**
 * Item superclass for the Antique Shop
 *
 * @author Kingsley Sage
 * @version 1.0
 */
public class Item
{
    public int value;
    public String creator;
}

public class Vase extends Item
{
    public int height;
    public String material;
}

public class Statue extends Item
{
    public int weight;
    public String colour;
}

public class Painting extends Item
{
    public int height;
    public int width;
    public boolean isWatercolour;
    public boolean isFramed;
}
```

If we create this as a project in BlueJ, we see the super and sub class relationship clearly on the central panel:

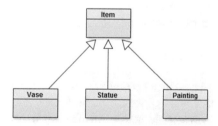

The Vase class has a total of four attributes. Two of these are unique to it, and two are "inherited" from its superclass. Similarly, the Painting class has six attributes, four unique to it, and two inherited from its superclass

So a super, base or parent class contains a basic set of attributes that are intended to form a part of the implementation of sub classes that are built from it. The sub classes have their own attributes that make them unique, and they inherit attributes from their superclass. Similarly, a sub class inherits methods from its super class. If we add a method to the super class `Item`, we find that instances of `Vase`, `Statue` and `Painting` will inherit it, and be able to call those inherited methods as if they had been defined in their own class definitions. In our example, a `showValue()` method has been added to the `Item` super class. A new `AntiqueShop` class has been created, and that creates `v1`, an object of type `Vase`, and `v1` then calls the new `showValue()` method:

```
// Method showValue() added to this class
public class Item
{
    public int value;
    public String creator;

    public void showValue()
    {
        System.out.println("This item is worth " +
            value + " pounds");
    }
}

public class AntiqueShop
{
    public Vase v1;

    public void addStock()
    {
        v1 = new Vase();
        v1.value = 100;
        v1.showValue(); // inherited from Item super class
    }
}
```

Note that, for now, all the attributes and methods have been declared as `public`. This is not necessarily good OO design practice and we return to this issue in Sect. 5.4.

The concept of inheritance can continue to be applied at further levels. We could sub class (extend) our sub classes again e.g. we could have different types of statue, vase or painting. They would then become super classes for the new sub classes and the rules of inheritance would apply throughout. In fact, it turns out that this is key to the very OO way Java is designed. All objects in Java, whether library or user-defined, ultimately share a common super class, the Java language base class `Object`. As such all objects inherit methods from `Object`. A good example of such a method is the `toString()` method. This is a method that determines what should be displayed on the console when `System.out.println()` is invoked. We can customise objects in this respect and we shall see this in Sect. 5.4 when we discuss over-riding.

5.3 Adding Constructors

We now know that inheritance allows sub classes to inherit attributes and methods from a super class. We now consider how we should build constructor methods so that instances of our sub classes are created in the most efficient manner.

As the sub class has access to all its attributes and methods, it is reasonable that each sub class could just provide its own full constructor, and we could forget about a constructor for the super class, as they are not, in general, intended to be instantiated directly. However, that is not efficient coding as it would involve code duplication. One reason why building super and sub classes is a good idea is the fact that we can reduce code duplication by factorising common attributes and methods into a single super class.

The solution is to provide the super class with a constructor in respect of its own attributes (and methods), and then create another constructor for each of the sub classes to deal with the attributes and methods that are unique to them. But that now means that there are two constructors to call; one for the super class and one for the sub class. We need to distinguish between these constructors and this is achieved using the super keyword. The super keyword refers to the super class of an object (as compared to the keyword this—the self-referential reference).

We use our antique shop example again to illustrate the point. Here a constructor has been added to the Item super class and a constructor has been added to the Vase sub class. Note that the Vase constructor takes a total of four parameters so that it can setup the object properly, and that it calls upon the Item constructor to deal with two of the attributes:

```
public class Item
{
    public int value;
    public String creator;

    public Item(int value, String creator)
    {
        this.value   = value;
        this.creator = creator;
    }
}

public class Vase extends Item
{
    public int height;
    public String material;

    public Vase(int value, String creator,
                int height, String material)
    {
        super(value, creator);
        this.height = height;
        this.material = material;
    }
}
```

If there are successive layers of super and sub classes, the same process can be extended so that the constructor of the lower sub class calls the constructor of its parent, that in turn calls its parent's constructor and so on until the object is fully constructed. There is only one other rule to be aware of:

Where a sub class is to call a constructor in its parent class using the super () method call, it must be so as the first line of its own constructor. This is to ensure that objects are constructed from their most distant super class first.

5.4 Rules of Inheritance and Over-Riding

Now that we understand the basic concept of inheritance, we can look at the rules that govern the actual process itself, as there are situations where we might wish to enact a more fine-grained control over what is inherited by a sub class from a super class. The first point to note is that any class can have at most only one parent class. Unlike other languages (notably C++) there is no concept of "multiple inheritance" from more than one direct super class. Classes cam inherit from a chain of super classes, but in each case only have one direct super class. C++ enthusiasts need not despair however as the Java concept of inheritance covered in Sect. 5.8 provides an alternative way of inheriting responsibilities from multiple classes.

In the example in Sect. 5.3, all the attributes and methods were declared as public. This is not generally good OO practice as we aspire to the principle of encapsulation. This suggests that attributes are, by design default, private unless there is a good reason otherwise. This presents a problem. If the attributes of a super class are private, then we cannot guarantee that they will be inherited by sub classes, as they are private to the super class. There are situations where it can happen, based on a more detailed analysis of the rules of inheritance when classes are distributed in different packages, but we shall not complicate the issue here.

What we need to do is to provide an alternative access modifier protected to go with the two existing modifiers private and public. The rules that govern how we can guarantee inheritance are as follows:

private: attributes and methods are only accessible from within the class itself, and are not guaranteed to be available in any class extended from it.

protected: attributes and methods that are private and only available from within the class itself and any class extended from it.

public: attributes and methods that are accessible from within the class and from any other class or calling code.

For our antique shop example, we should set the attributes to protected in the super class Item, and the attributes to private in the sub classes. The constructor in the super class remains public and should always be so.

That provides an elegant solution for the encapsulation issue. But what about situations where we don't necessarily want to inherit the version of a method from the super class, but instead replace it with something else. Such a situation requires an "override". The idea is that when we make a method call, we look at the immediate class definition for a method that matches our call. If one is found, we invoke that method. If no matching method is found, we turn to the super class. If one is found there, we involve it. If no matching method is found, we continue to move through the chain of super classes until we either find a method that matches, or we reach the Java language base class Object and have still not found a match, and the compiler will report that no matching method can be found.

For our sub classes, we can choose to override a method inherited from the super class by simply defining a new method with the name and pattern of formal parameters. By coding convention, and to give other programmers notice that we are doing so, we annotate the overriding method using the @Override annotation.

For our antique shop example, let's say that we want the showValue() method in the Vase class to be different in implementation to the one inherited from Item. But we do want Statue and Painting to inherit the one from Item as before. So we leave the class definitions of Statue and Painting unchanged, and add an overriding method definition in the Vase class. Putting these new ideas into our example, our code base now looks like this:

```
/**
 * AntiqueShop example refined
 *
 * @author Kingsley Sage
 * @version 1.0
 */

public class AntiqueShop
{
    private Vase v1;
    private Painting p1;

    public void addStock()
    {
        v1 = new Vase(0,"Dave", 50, "bronze");
        v1.showValue();
        p1 = new Painting(100, "John",true, false, 50,25);
        p1.showValue();
    }
}

public class Item
{
    protected int value;
    protected String creator;

    public Item(int value, String creator)
    {
        this.value  = value;
        this.creator = creator;
    }
    protected void showValue()
    {
        System.out.println("This item is worth " +
                            value + " pounds");
    }
}

public class Vase extends Item
{
    private int height;
    private String material;

    public Vase(int value, String creator,
                int height, String material)
    {
        super(value, creator);
        this.height = height;
        this.material = material;
    }
```

```
    @Override
    public void showValue()
    {
        if (value > 0)
        {
            System.out.println("This vase is worth " +
                                    value + " pounds");
        }
        else
        {
            System.out.println("Vase value not yet determined");
        }
    }
}

public class Statue extends Item
{
    private int weight;
    private String colour;

    public Statue(int value, String creator,
                  int weight, String colour)
    {
        super(value, creator);
        this.weight = weight;
        this.colour = colour;
    }
}

public class Painting extends Item
{
    private int height;
    private int width;
    private boolean isWatercolour;
    private boolean isFramed;

    public Painting(int value, String creator,
                    boolean isWatercolour, boolean isFramed,
                    int height, int width)
    {
        super(value, creator);
        this.height = height;
        this.isWatercolour = isWatercolour;
        this.isFramed = isFramed;
        this.height = height;
        this.width = width;
    }
}
```

In the `AntiqueShop` class, we create a `Vase v1` and a `Painting p1`. When we call the `showValue()` method, `v1` draw upon the override method version in its own class definition, but `p1` draws upon the version inherited from `Item`. Thus we can exert fine grained control over what method versions are called in any situation.

For completeness, here is the class diagram as shown on the BlueJ central panel:

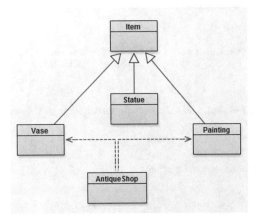

We see the super and sub classes relationships as before, but we also see the dotted arrows between AntiqueShop, Vase and Painting. This is an "association" relationship and simply denotes that AntiqueShop is making use of Vase and Painting, in the sense that it has declared references to them, and thus there is a dependency.

5.5 Method Polymorphism

We have explored the idea that classes can appear in many forms. But the concept of polymorphism does not end there. Methods can also appear in many different forms. A good example here would be a constructor method. The job of a constructor method is to initialise an object. Depending on what data is available at the time the object is created, it may need to be initialised in different ways. More than one constructor can be created to deal with the different scenarios. They must all carry the same method name as their class, or they would not be categorised as constructor methods But they will need to differ in the pattern and/or number of formal parameters so that the compiler can work out which of the constructors is the correct one to call.

Using our antique shop example once, let's equip the Vase class with two constructors. One when we know all the attribute values (as before) and another where we only know the height and material:

```
public Vase(int value, String creator,
            int height, String material)
{
    super(value, creator);
    this.height = height;
    this.material = material;
}

public Vase(int height, String material)
{
    super(0,"unkwown");
    this.height = height;
    this.material = material;
}
```

We say that the Vase constructor method is polymorphic as it appears in two forms. We can describe the form using the method signatures:

```
Vase(int, String, int, String)
Vase(int, String)
```

When we instantiate instances of the Vase object, the compiler will look for a matching constructor signature. Each signature must be unique or the compiler will report an error. If the compiler cannot locate a matching signature, it will report an error. So in our AntiqueShop class, we now have two options to creates Vase objects:

```
v1 = new Vase(0,"Dave", 50, "bronze");
v1.showValue();
v2 = new Vase(100,"plaster");
v2.showValue();
```

Method polymorphism also extends to general methods. We can have as many alternative implementations of a method as we like as long as they are all unique in their signature of formal parameters. Note that uniqueness by returned value type alone is not sufficient. So, we could create two trimPainting() methods in our Painting class:

```
public void trimPainting()
{
    width -= 1;
}

public void trimPainting(int amount)
{
    width -= amount;
}
```

The first version is for when we have not been given a value for the amount to reduce the width, and thus use a default value of 1. The second can be used where we have been given an amount to reduce the width by.

5.6   Static and Dynamic Type

We have seen already the nature of the relationship between super classes and their sub classes. We now delve a little deeper into Java to understand the precise nature of object type. On the face of it, an object has the type that was declare for it, but that is not quite the full story, as it does not take into account the is-a relationship.

An object can have more than one type:

static type: the type that it has when first declared. Static type checking is enforced by the compiler. This should not be confused with the use of the static keyword that we consider later.

dynamic type: the type that is has at runtime.

To make things clear consider this following code building on the antique shop example:

```
v1 = new Vase(0,"Dave", 50, "bronze");
Item i1 = v1;
```

Object v1 has a static type of Vase. But object i1 has a static type of Item and a dynamic type of Vase. This is possible because v1 is a Vase, but it is also an Item.

This might not seem very useful, but in fact it helps us solve a problem. Our AntiqueShop could really use a collection of all the artefacts that it has. But these things could be any mixture of objects of type Vase, Statue and Painting. We could use 3 separate ArrayList collections. We know that an ArrayList must be a collection of a single type. But that is not convenient coding and requires a deal of code duplication. In reality the shop really has is a collection of objects of common type Item. So we could have an ArrayList of type Item. Objects of type Vase, Status and Painting all have the possibility of a dynamic type of Item, so can be added to a single collection ArrayList of type Item.

We now further refine the AntiqueShop in exactly this way:

```
import java.util.*;

/**
 * AntiqueShop example with ArrayList
 *
 * @author Kingsley Sage
 * @version 1.0
 */
public class AntiqueShop
{
    private ArrayList<Item> allItems;

    public AntiqueShop()
    {
        allItems = new ArrayList<Item>();
    }

    public void addStock()
    {
        Vase v1 = new Vase(0,"Dave", 50, "bronze");
        Painting p1 = new Painting(100, "John",true,
                                   false, 50,25);
        Statue s1 = new Statue(1000,"Sheila",20,"orange");
        allItems.add(v1);
        allItems.add(p1);
        allItems.add(s1);
    }
}
```

This is an elegant and practical solution for the AntiqueShop as it now needs only one collection to do its job. This example does raise a further issue though. What should we do if we want to create a method to iterate through the ArrayList and display details about each item in the shop?

One obvious solution would be to provide each class with a displayDetails() method. That can certainly be done, but it not quite satisfactory in that if the method was common to all the sub-classes, then OO design philosophy would suggest that the method definition belongs in the Item super class.

5.7   Abstract Classes

We have previously discussed that super classes tend to be more abstract in their nature than the more concrete sub classes. The abstract nature is a reflection of the fact that they are OO design constructs intended as a means of avoiding code duplication, and of modelling some real-world problem domain in a more reflective manner.

In the previous section, we noted that if we wanted to have a `displayDetails()` method, then by design it should be common to all classes and thus the obvious place for it is within the super class `Item`, so that it can be duly inherited by all the sub classes. But this is not possible in practice as the sub classes have attributes that are `private` to them, and are not known or accessible by their parent super class. So a method in `Item` cannot access the `Vase` attributes.

What we can say is that, conceptually at least, `displayDetails()` would belong in `Item`, it's just that `Item` is not able to provide the implementation. This is where we meet the notion of an abstract method.

An **abstract method** is a signature definition of a method but with no implementation. The implementation of the method falls to any class that extends the class that defined the abstract method.

First, let's add the definition of the `abstract` method to `Item`:

```
public abstract class Item
{
    protected int value;
    protected String creator;

    // Other methods omitted for brevity

    public abstract void displayDetails();

}
```

Note also the addition of the `abstract` keyword in the class definition itself. The `Item` class has become an `abstract` class.

An **abstract class** is a class that contains one or more `abstract` method definitions.

Our attention now turns to the sub classes. As they extend `Item`, they inherit the `abstract` definition of the `displayDetails()` method. They are now required to provide a concrete implementation of that method. The compiler will not regard the sub class definitions as complete until they provide such a concrete implementation. So, using the `Vase` class as an example:

```
public void displayDetails()
{
    System.out.println("This vase was created by " + creator);
    System.out.println("It has a value of " + value
                       + " pounds");
    System.out.println("It is " + height + " cm tall");
    System.out.println("It is made of " + material);
}
```

We are obliged to similarly equip the `Statue` and `Painting` sub classes:

```
// In the Statue class
    public void displayDetails()
    {
        System.out.println("This statue was created by "
                           + creator);
        System.out.println("It has a value of " + value +
                           " pounds");
        System.out.println("It weighs " + weight + " kg");
        System.out.println("It is " + colour + " in colour");
    }

// In the Painting class

    public void displayDetails()
    {
        System.out.println("This paining was created by " +
                           creator);
        System.out.println("It has a value of " + value +
                           " pounds");
        if (isWatercolour == true)
        {
            System.out.println("It is a watercolour");
        }
        if (isFramed == true)
        {
            System.out.println("It is a framed picture");
        }
        else
        {
            System.out.println("It is an unframed picture");
        }
        System.out.println("The height is " + height + " cm");
        System.out.println("The width is " + width + " cm");
    }
```

So we have a general principle:

> A **sub class is only complete** once it has provided concrete implementations
> of all `abstract` methods inherited from its parent super class/classes.

The use of `abstract` methods provides us with a guarantee of the capabilities
of a sub class. That is useful as now we can rely on such methods in our
`AntiqueShop`. We can create a method in `AntiqueShop` to iterate through the
`ArrayList` collection of `Item`, and call the `displayDetails()` method for
each in turn:

```
public void showAllStock()
{
    for (Item i: allItems)
    {
        i.displayDetails();
    }
}
```

5.8 Interfaces

Some OO languages, notably C++, support the notion of multiple inheritance
whereby a class can inherit attributes and methods from more than one parent class.
This can lead to some challenges where attributes and methods of the same name
are to be inherited from different places. Java only permits inheritance from one
direct parent class. However, there are situations where it is desirable to able to take
on responsibilities from other classes. This is achieved through the concept of an
interface.

As the name suggests, an interface provides a single consistent specification of
some functionality that a class is intended to provide. A Java interface can only
contain method signatures and fields. It cannot, in general, contain an implementation of the methods. This makes an interface look like an abstract class where all
of the methods are abstract. A class can then opt to implement the interface. The
implementing class is then obliged to provide a concrete implementation of the
interface methods. To create an interface in BlueJ, select the "New Class" option,
but set the radio button to "Interface". Here is an example interface:

```
public interface MyInterface
{
    // An example of an interface attribute
    public String defaultMessage = "Hello World";

    // Interface method
    public void displayMessage();
}
```

The use of interface attributes is somewhat limited, but you can access them directly from the interface if you need to:

```
System.out.println(MyInterface.defaultMessage);
```

Now we can make a class that implements the interface. Rather than extending a parent class as before, we implement the interface:

```
public class Message implements MyInterface
{
    private String content;
    private String from;
    private String to;

    public void displayMessage()
    {
        content = "Fish ";
        System.out.println(content);
    }
}
```

The idea is that other classes might also implement the same interface. How they do it is up to them. One class may display the message on the console (as above), another might place the message on a GUI panel, another may send the message over a network. But if they all implement the same interface, we are guaranteed that they do provide an implementation of displayMessage().

You cannot create an instance of the interface on its own—that would make no sense as it is essentially an abstract entity. But you can require a class to implement multiple interfaces:

```
public class Message implements MyInterface, AnotherInterface
{
    / / Content in here …
}
```

All methods in an interface are public. If you omit the access modifier, the method will still be public. By allowing classes to implement multiple interfaces, we can achieve most of the desirable elements of traditional multiple inheritance. A class may extend a parent class and implement as many interfaces as it needs to do its job.

A recent innovation from Java 8 is the notion that the interface can provide a default implementation of interface methods. This can be helpful in the sense that there may be situations where two classes may utilise the same implementation of one of the interface methods. If the implementing class does not provide its concrete implementation of the interface method, the it will take on the default implementation from the interface:

```java
public interface MyInterface
{
    // An example of an interface attribute
    public String defaultMessage = "Hello World";

    // Interface methods
    public void displayMessage();

    default String appendToMessage(String msg, String msg2)
    {
        // Concatenate the two strings
        return msg + msg2;
    }
}
```

Note the use of the default keyword in the interface method. Any implementation in a class that implements an interface will override a default interface method.

Now our Message class might look like this:

```java
public class Message implements MyInterface
{
    private String content;
    private String from;
    private String to;

    public void displayMessage()
    {
        content = "Fish ";
        System.out.println(content);
        System.out.println(appendToMessage(content, "and chips"));
    }
}
```

It is also possible for interfaces to be organised as super and sub interfaces, with interfaces inheriting from one another. But that is making things too complex for now.

5.9   Class Variables and Static Methods

We have seen that objects are unique instances of some class type. The class definition specifies the attributes and methods that an object will have. Each instance of that class is its own object of that class type. Object attributes are frequently referred to as instance variables. But it is also possible to create variables that are shared by all instances of a class. These are referred to as "class variables".

> A **class variable** is declared as a **static** variable in the class definition. There is only one copy of the static variable and it is shared by all instances of that class. If any object alters the value of that static variable, the change is visible to all instances of that class.

The use of static variables is somewhat limited in practice. It can be used, for example to keep track of how many instances of a class have been instantiated:

```
public class Item
{
    private String name;
    static int numInstances = 0;

    public Item(String name)
    {
        this.name = name;
        numInstances++;
    }

    public void displayNumberOfInstanes()
    {
        System.out.println(numInstances);
    }
}
```

However, it is trickier to determine when an object has gone out of scope, and thus that numInstances should be decreased. This is because there it is not up to the user to determine when an object in memory is no longer required and can be disposed of. This is determined by the JVM which is lazy in its garbage collection.

Rather more useful is the idea that we can use static variables to hold constants. This provides us with a practical means of storing global values. This can be conveniently achieved using the concept of a static, or utility class.

A static method is one that can be invoked even though no instance of the class was ever instantiated. This may seem odd, but it is useful in situations where the content of the method has no dependency on any instance variables or other non-static methods. For example:

```
public class UtilityClass
{
    public static int VITAL_CONSTANT = 42;

    public static int addTwoNumbers(int x, int y)
    {
        return x+y;
    }
}
```

Clearly, addTwoNumbers() is entirely self-contained and does not rely on any other class infrastructure. So it can be summoned even though the class it belongs to has not been instantiated. Maths functions are a good example of a whole category of methods that do not really need to belong to any particular class to do their job. In reality, they are like C functions. They exist as static methods in a class solely because the OO nature of Java requires them to belong to some class, even if they have no thematic connection with that class. It is often convenient to group methods together:

> A static **class** is one that contains only static attributes and/or static methods.

Probably the most often used static class in Java is the Math class. As it is not intended to be instantiated by the user, we refer to it by its class name. So in the example above we access the constant by UtilityClass.VITAL_CONSTANT and the method as UtilityClass.addTwoNumbers(). By convention, constants in utility classes are written in upper case e.g. Math.PI.

There is one other notable use of a static method and that is main(). Up to this point, we have been responsible for creating instances of classes in BlueJ and invoking an appropriate method to get the work done. But in real world applications we operate outside of the BlueJ environment. So a Java application needs a means of knowing how to start itself. But this requires Java to instantiate an object and call a method. This is where the main() comes in. In a Java project, one and only one of the classes is nominated as being the host of a main() method. The main() method is declared as static. When the program is to be executed, the JVM identifies which of the classes has the main() method and executes it. It can do this as the method is static. Typically the main() method then creates an instance of one of the classes (usually the one it resides in) and calls a method to initiate the application. You can think of `main()` as being like a flag on a golf course that tells the player where to begin playing!

```
public class Game
{
    private int x,y;

    public Game()
    {
        System.out.println("Instance up and running");
    }

    public void method1()
    {
        // Some useful code ...
    }

    public static void main(String[] args)
    {
        Game g1 = new Game();
        g1.method1();
    }
}
```

The signature of the `main()` method is always `public void static main (String[] args)`. The formal parameter is an array of type `String`. Although little used in a world of Graphical User Interfaces (GUIs), the array of `String` represents an optional set of console command line options that can be specified when launching a Java application in a text only console window.

You can still implement the `main()` method whilst working in the BlueJ environment. But rather than instantiating an object and calling one of its methods as before, you can just right click the class on the central panel and call the `main()` method directly.

At this point, you should be feeling comfortable with the concept of OO coding, and able to see the value that it brings in modelling real world problems. But we are not expert coders yet! Really good programs work even in challenging conditions, and when dealing with poor user input or incomplete information. In the next chapter we start to explore how to make our code more resilient in the face of errors.

Dealing with Errors

6

It is inevitable when producing any non-trivial software project that we will encounter errors, unexpected eventualities and erroneous data. This is just a fact of life and we need to develop strategies for dealing with it. Given that our modern world is so dependent on software systems, it highlights the need to design and produce software systems that are as free from error as possible, and that react predictably and robustly when things don't go as expected. In this chapter we explore how to deal with errors in a wide range of scenarios and we develop a number of approaches to try to ensure that we don't end up staring at a screen with little or no understanding of why things are not happening the way we intended.

6.1 The Nature of Errors

Anyone involved in teaching coding will have heard the immortal claim by a student that "*my program isn't working correctly*". Well, the news is that it is – it just isn't doing what you intended. Computers and compilers are very useful, but they are not mind readers and they can only perform the precise task that the code specifies. Programming languages have a syntax that follows strict and precise rules so that there is a single and unambiguous execution path. The main source of problem conditions with modern software tends to be the user. Users make errors in providing data input, and often fail to read the instructions on how to use the software. Nonetheless the software is expected to work "correctly" in these conditions.

It is worth considering a taxonomy of sources of errors as it helps us to consider what broad approach is right in dealing with any specific problem we may encounter. Some are relatively easy to fix and some may prove more challenging. It is also worth considering whether it is, in fact, ever possible to produce a piece of

© Springer Nature Switzerland AG 2019
K. Sage, *Concise Guide to Object-Oriented Programming*,
Undergraduate Topics in Computer Science,
https://doi.org/10.1007/978-3-030-13304-7_6

software that is guaranteed 100% free from error. The answer is a simple "no" even for small programs. If we build a small program, even one as simple as the classic "Hello World", we are using tools and applications that we did not create and have no guarantees of provenance. How do we know that the compiler that we use does not have some obscure error? Software systems such as operating systems, compilers, libraries and support applications are the subject of continuous improvement and updates. There have been many real-world cases where such updates have caused whole categories of software systems to malfunction or even fail altogether, sometimes with little thought given as to how to roll back to a safer previous version.

When a piece of software is developed it is subjected to a testing regime. During the initial phases of that regime errors will be discovered easily and will be fixed. But as time passes, errors will become more infrequent and difficult to diagnose. As such, the cost of fixing them increases. Ultimately there may be errors that occur so infrequently that despite months of testing, they do not show themselves, but once the code is deployed, they will eventually do so. This implies that an infinite amount of time is required to ensure that software is 100% free from error, and that is neither practical nor economic to do so. So we must accept that software can have errors and work in a manner intended to mitigate the consequences. That's a sobering though for those involved in the design of software systems for avionics, but it is the reality. A common question that arises in software development is therefore "how much effort should I put into ensuring that my software is free from errors?" The answer depends entirely on what the software is being used for, and what the consequences would be of unexpected failure. It is, at most, inconvenient if our latest trend social media application stops working. But in avionics control, the consequences are much more severe and potentially life threatening. Interestingly, there are three stand out industries that put a huge effort into software reliability; avionics, medical systems and the games industry. The latter might seem unlikely, but it is worth reflecting that as modern computer games are multi-million pound investments by development houses, and that no return on that investment is achieved until you sell copies of the finished produced, most games software development houses are one poorly received title away from economic ruin.

Errors can occur in all phases of a software application's lifecycle:

Coding syntax errors: the code produced does not compile as the rules of the language have not been followed properly. The responsibility lies with the developer to remedy these errors.

Logic errors: the code compiles, but does not function in the intended manner. Typically these errors occur as the developer has made a mistake when producing the code. Testing usually exposes these errors, and they are relatively easy to fix. We associate this kind of error with the process of "debugging".

Design errors: the code works fine but does not address the requirements of the user. This can be a very costly type of error to address, and usually comes about because the developer has not understood the needs of the end user properly. Design errors are the consequence of poor software engineering practice, and can, in extreme cases, cause failure of the project as a whole.

User errors: the code works, but does not respond consistently or coherently when faced with erroneous user input. For example, the code askes the user to "select a menu option from 1 to 5" and the user enters 6. Did the software provide a useful error message, or instead pursue some unknown default value? This type of error is addressed through unit and system level testing. Developers often under-estimate the time it can take to harden a piece of software against user errors. Defensive coding is a typical means of dealing with this type of error.

Run time errors: for example failure to open external assets such as files, network connections that do not respond in a timely manner and faults in run time support infrastructure such as the JVM running out of memory. We usually deal with these errors using exception handling.

Environmental errors: errors that arise due to factors outside the immediate scope of the application such as hardware failure. There is often little we can do about these issues, other than ensure that our software closes down in an orderly manner.

Dealing with syntax coding errors at the compile stage is the easiest – for a compiled language such as Java we can't make deploy the application until these errors are dealt with, and solving them just requires knowledge and patience. However, for interpreted languages such as JavaScript this is not the case. For the interpreted scripting languages we don't detect even these basic syntax errors until we try to run the code.

For all other types or source of error, we need to consider what strategies we can bring to bear to minimise them happening, and deal with them when they do.

6.2   Coding Defensively

The art of coding defensively reflects the adage that "prevention is better than cure". In coding terms, this means working to prevent erroneous data from propagating through our application. Defensive coding refers to a style of working where:

- Checks are applied at the earliest opportunity to ensure that data is valid.
- Attribute values can only be set (mutated) in a controlled way.
- Default conditions are set in place for control constructions to ensure that there is always a directed path of execution.
- Only those attributes and methods that need to be `public` are declared as such.

We already learned about mutator methods in Chap. 3. One of the real benefits of using a mutator method is that it allows us to control precisely how a `private` instance variable should be set. Consider the following very basic mutator:

```
private int x;

public void setX(int x)
{
    this.x = x;
}
```

The `setX()` mutator provides external access to the x attribute. But here there is not really much benefit in the mutator method, since we could still use it to set x to any value. What if it was essential that x only ever had a value in the range 0 to 10 (inclusive):

```
public void setX(int x)
{
    if ((x >= 0) && (x <= 10))
    {
        this.x = x;
    }
}
```

Here we make use of a conditional `if` statement to safeguard the integrity of x. If we try to set an invalid value, x simply remains at its previous value. Note however it would still be possible to set x to an invalid value using direct access to x from within the defining class.

The design of conditional statements themselves should also embrace defensive coding. In our example above, if we did try to set an invalid value for x, we would be unaware that it had in fact remained at its original value. This is because there is no `else` condition in the conditional statement. You can think of `else` as a strategy to be pursued when no other options are the right one. Here, a simple message to the user might be appropriate:

```
public void setX(int x)
{
    if ((x >= 0) && (x <= 10))
    {
        this.x = x;
    }
    else
    {
        System.out.println("Invalid x");

    }
}
```

Good coding will generally see `if` statements have an `else` condition, and `switch` statements with a default `case` option.

Turning to repetition structures, we need to ensure that it is always possible for the controlling test condition to fail so that the loop will eventually terminate, otherwise we have the potential for an infinite loop. When iterating through a collection such as an `ArrayList`, we should use a structure that either uses the `size()` method to dynamically determine the list size, or use the alternative form of iteration.

Poor coding would separate the record of the length from the collection:

```
import java.util.*;

public class DefensiveCoding
{
    private int x;
    private ArrayList<String> someList;

    public void poorCoding()
    {
        int x;
        ArrayList<String> someList;

        someList = new ArrayList<String>();
        someList.add("crocodile");
        someList.add("gnu");
        x = 2;

        for (int y=0; y<x; y++)
        {
            System.out.println(someList.get(y));
        }

    }
}
```

The danger here is that x and the length of the `ArrayList` become unsynchronised. A better solution would be:

```
import java.util.*;

public class DefensiveCoding
{
    private int x;
    private ArrayList<String> someList;

    public void betterCoding()
    {

        someList = new ArrayList<String>();
        someList.add("crocodile");
        someList.add("gnu");

        for (int y=0; y<someList.size(); y++)
        {
            System.out.println(someList.get(y));
        }

        for (String s: someList)
        {
            System.out.println(s);
        }
    }
}
```

These are just some basic examples of a defensive coding style. They are reflections of just plain good coding style along with the use of appropriate commenting, sensible variable names, task decomposition, cohesion and encapsulation.

6.3   Using the Debugger Tool

Even once we have embraced the concept of defensive coding, errors will still occur. Some of these will be logic errors, where the developer has just plain got the code wrong and has not implemented what they thought. Such errors require a strategy to solve them. The simplest approach is the "structured walkthrough" of a piece of code, working one line at a time seeing whether the expected behaviour matches the actual behaviour of the code. Many beginner programmers make extensive use of System.out.println() to do this. That's OK for a while, but it is problematic as it can bloat the codebase making it harder to see what it going on, and also it means that we have to interfere with the codebase to test it. Ideally, we need a means of looking inside the software as it executes to see what is happening. We have already seen in Chap. 3 the BlueJ inspector which is useful in seeing what values attributes have. To use the inspector, we can right click objects on the workbench and select "inspect":

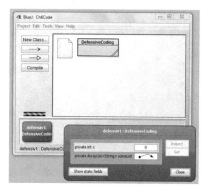

The inspector is a very useful tool, and is not limited to just examining a single attribute. We can also "drill down" through objects to examine all aspects of their inner state. For example, we see that the `ArrayList someList` has a curved arrow to show us an object reference to a contained object. We can click on the arrow to drill down into `someList` and see its value:

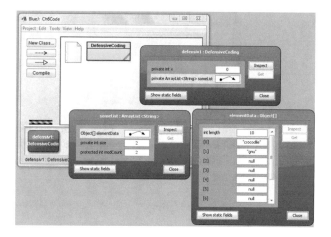

This is a superior approach to just using `System.out.println()` as we don't need to modify the codebase to see what is happening within. But this approach is only useful if the object we want to inspect is actually on the work-bench. But objects created programmatically within the code do not appear on the workbench. In this scenario, we need a more powerful tool than the Inspector and this is where the debugger comes in.

A **debugger** allows for the testing of a target program. A debugger allows the code to be executed in blocks or at a line at a time as if the code was interpreted. A debugger will facilitate the setting of **breakpoints** at specific lines of code, allow the user to examine variable values and the state of the **call stack**. This permits the results of the code execution to be compared with the developer's expectations to determine whether the code is functioning as intended.

To expose the debugger window in Blue J select "Show debugger" from the View menu tab:

The call stack is show on the "call sequence" panel. The variable panels will display the values of all variables in scope at any point in the debugging workflow. To debug a program you will need to set one or more breakpoints. These are set in the source code editor window:

```java
someList = new ArrayList<String>();
someList.add("crocodile");
someList.add("gnu");

for (int y=0; y<someList.size(); y++)
{
    System.out.println(someList.get(y));
}
```

On the white strip to the left of the code, click the mouse to set and unset points in the code where you want execution to pause. Note that these breakpoints must be on lines of code that do something, they cannot be set, for example, on a line with just a brace on it. You can have as many breakpoints as you need. Then run your code as normal. When the program reaches a breakpoint, the debugger window will open:

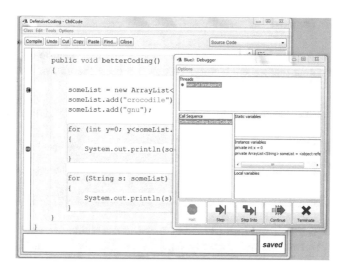

We see that the calls sequence specifies that we are in DefensiveCoding at method betterCoding(). We can see our instance variables. Any further local variables would also be displayed. We can click on object variable names and the Inspector will open up (very useful as the objects no longer need to reside on the workbench). We now have the option to:

- Execute the next line of code.
- Execute the next line, but if that statement contains a method invocation, then the program will enter the method and wait for further user interaction.
- Continue execution to the next breakpoint, or the program exits of its own accord, whichever occurs first.
- Terminate the current program execution.

You should take some time to get used to the debugger as you will find, over time, that it is one of the most useful tools in figuring out why a program is not behaving the way you intended.

It is worth observing that whilst the debugger is a great tool for identifying logic errors, design errors are a much harder problem to solve. The greatest tool is getting the design right is you, experience, a pen and paper and taking the time to really think about what you are trying to achieve.

6.4   Unit Testing

Once you have created a program that you think is functioning properly, it's time to expose it to some methodical testing. Testing can be at the unit or system level.

> **Unit level testing**: individual classes are tested to ensure that they function according to their cohesive purpose. Sometimes small groups of classes are tested working together - this is referred to as component level testing.
>
> **System level testing**: where a program as a whole is checked to see that it operates as intended.

As an analogy, if we were building a car, we would first check that each individual element worked correctly e.g. the engine, the transmission and the entertainment system. Only once we were satisfied that each component worked correctly, we would assemble them together to make the complete system and then take it for a system level test drive.

In an OO language, unit level testing is usually associated with making sure individual classes operate correctly. We want to do this in a manner that does not disturb the underlying code base. In Java, we can create unit test classes.

> A **unit test class** is a class contained in a project that permits automated testing of one or more classes, but the test class itself does not form part of the actual functional codebase.

To create a unit test class in BlueJ, select "New class" and then select the "Unit Test" option. By convention, unit test classes are named by the class they test coupled with the word Test. To help us understand unit test classes in practice, we will use the following BookReviews class:

```java
import java.util.*;

/**
 * A class to store reviews of a Book
 *
 * @author Kingsley Sage
 * @version 1.0
 */
public class BookReviews
{
    private ArrayList<String> allReviews;
    private double rating;
    private String bookTitle;
    private String bookAuthor;

    public BookReviews(String bookTitle, String bookAuthor)
    {
        this.bookTitle = bookTitle;
        this.bookAuthor = bookAuthor;
        rating = 0.0;
        allReviews = new ArrayList<String>();
    }

    /**
     * A method to add a review to the list of reviews.
     * @param String with the text of the review
     * @param int with the rating out of 5
     * @return true if the review was accepted
     */
    public boolean addReview(String review, int myRating)
    {
        if ((myRating < 0) || (myRating > 5))
        {
            System.out.println("Rating must in range 0 to 5");
            return false;
        }
        else if (review.isEmpty()==true)
        {
            System.out.println("Review text is empty");
            return false;
        }
        else
        {
            allReviews.add(review);
            // Update the average score
            if (allReviews.size() == 1)
            {
                rating = (double) myRating;
            }
            else
            {
                double x = rating * (allReviews.size()-1);
                x = x + (double) myRating;
                rating = x / allReviews.size();
```

```
            }
            return true;
        }
    }

    /**
     * A method to display all reviews and the average rating.
     * @param none
     * @return none
     */
    public void displayReviews()
    {
        if (allReviews.size() > 0)
        {
            for (String r:allReviews)
            {
                System.out.println(r);
            }
            // Display rating to 2 decimal places
            System.out.println("Current rating: " +
                               String.format("%.2f",rating));
        }
        else
        {
            System.out.println("No reviews yet");
        }
    }

}
```

The concept here is that we can enter a review and a rating only if:

- The rating is between 0 and 5 inclusive.
- The review is not empty text.

This seems easy enough, and the code has compiled. But is the code free from error, and does it do exactly what was intended? We could create an instance of the class and call the various methods manually. But instead we create a unit test class called `BookReviewsTest`. It will appear in the Java central panel as a green box (to remind us that it does not form a part of the main codebase). If we open the test class in the code editor, we find quite a lot of useful code has been generated automatically:

```java
import static org.junit.Assert.*;
import org.junit.After;
import org.junit.Before;
import org.junit.Test;

/**
 * The test class BookReviewsTest.
 *
 * @author  Kingsley Sage
 * @version 1.0
 */
public class BookReviewsTest
{
    /**
     * Default constructor for test class BookReviewsTest
     */
    public BookReviewsTest()
    {
    }

    /**
     * Sets up the test fixture.
     *
     * Called before every test case method.
     */
    @Before
    public void setUp()
    {
    }

    /**
     * Tears down the test fixture.
     *
     * Called after every test case method.
     */
    @After
    public void tearDown()
    {
    }
}
```

Note the use of several Java annotations. In all we have:

- A constructor for the test class.
- A blank method called setUp() annotated with @Before. Any method annotated as @Before will be executed after the constructor but before each and every actual test is carried out.
- A blank method called teardown() annotated with @After. Any method annotated as @After will be executed after each test has been carried out.

The test class is much like any other class in that it can have attributes and other non-annotated methods. We don't have to use the constructor, or the @Before and @After parts, but they can be helpful in larger test arrangements.

We shall create our first test. Tests are created as methods annotated with @Test. Out first test will create an instance of the BookReviews class and add one properly formed review to it:

```
@Test
public void test1()
{
    BookReviews b1 = new BookReviews("fishing", "smith");
    assertEquals(
        b1.addReview("A splendid read - highly recommended",5),
        true);
}
```

The assertEquals() method is the key. The first argument is out method call to our object b1. We know that addReview() will return true if all is well. The second argument is the value we expect addReview() to return – if it does that it is working fine.

Now that we have a test, we just need to run it. It wc now look at BlueJ, we see:

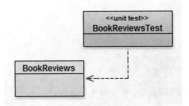

Now we right click on the unit test class where we have options to "Test all" or invoke "test1()" as we have defined it. It is more pleasing to select "Test all" and when we do we see:

We see that the test was conducted and the class has a green clear bill of health based on the current test set. If `assertEquals()` found a different result to the one expected, a red band would be displayed instead. So, is our code perfect?

Let's try adding a blank review. We can see that the code already should deal with a blank `String` when invoking `addReview()`, but is it foolproof? Let's reorganise our test class:

```java
import static org.junit.Assert.*;
import org.junit.After;
import org.junit.Before;
import org.junit.Test;

/**
 * The test class BookReviewsTest.
 *
 * @author  Kingsley Sage
 * @version 1.1
 */
public class BookReviewsTest
{
    private BookReviews b1;
    /**
     * Default constructor for test class BookReviewsTest
     */
    public BookReviewsTest()
    {
        b1 = new BookReviews("fishing", "smith");
    }

    @Test
    public void test1()
    {
        assertEquals(
            b1.addReview("A splendid read - highly recommended",5),
            true);
    }

    @Test
    public void blankStringTest()
    {
        assertEquals(b1.addReview("  ",0), false);
    }

}
```

Once again, we select "Test all" for the unit test class and we find that `blankStringTest()` has failed, as the methods has returned `true` when we were expecting `false`. If we click on the red test result we will get a summary explanation:

The problem here is a logic problem. We used the `isEmpty()` method from the `String` class to determine if the user entered a blank review. But in the test case we use a `String` that actually consisted of some white space – blank but not an empty `String`. What we need to do is to trim the input `String` before evaluating whether it is indeed empty. We can do this by just changing one line in the `BookReview` class:

```
// else if (review.isEmpty()==true)
// replace with

else if (review.trim().isEmpty()==true)
```

The `trim()` method is invoked prior to `isEmpty()`. Now we re-run all tests and find that we have passed.

We can continue to build as many tests as we think are required to demonstrate that the software is "fit for purpose". It is up to us as developers to determine that fitness. Professional software teams often have a dedicated test engineer writing test scripts. The automated nature of these tests means that we can carry on incrementally developing code and adding to our classes, safe in the knowledge that as our bank of tests builds up, we always have a means of checking whether some code we added has caused a problem in our existing codebase. Once we have finished our classes, we have a means of providing assurance that the class operates correctly. Some professionals advocate "Test Driven Development" (TDD) where the tests any class must pass are defined at the outset prior to the body of the class ever being written. Development then continues until the class can pass all of its tests.

There is much to the topic of automated testing, and we have just touched on some of the most important aspects, but you should be left with a desire to investigate how unit testing can be incorporated into your everyday workflow as a means of developing a more robust codebase.

6.5 System Testing

Once we are satisfied that each individual class is working correctly, the next phase of testing in software engineering involves testing the application as a whole. The system testing process is often a part automated process and part a case of building a documented process.

At the automated level, it is perfectly possible to create Java unit test classes that run the entire application – there is no particular constraint on what objects a unit test class can create and the methods that it can call. But the extent to which this is practical depends on the design of the application itself, particularly in respect of any user interface aspects of the application. For example, if the application requires user input, it can be difficult to create a test class that fully simulates the user interaction. The user would still be required to enter whatever data was necessary to make the application run.

One strategy for dealing with this is to add additional methods to the codebase that are only there to assist in automated system level testing. Such methods allow for the "injection" of user input in lieu of any user interface code. Whilst this solves the problem of automating the tests, it does mean that the code is not being tested quite "as is". For example, in the code example below there is a method to allow for some user input using the Scanner class. To facilitate testing, an alternative method is provided that can achieve the same effect, but under code control without the Scanner class:

```java
import java.util.*;

/**
 * An example of how to adapt code to facilitate
 * automated system level testing.
 *
 * @author Kingsley Sage
 * @version 1.0
 */
public class TestingExample
{
    private int x;

    /**
     * Enters a value for x using Scanner
     */
    public void userEntersValue()
    {
        Scanner sc = new Scanner(System.in);
        System.out.println("Enter a value for x:");
        x = sc.nextInt();
    }

    /**
     * Alternative for automated system testing
     * @param int value of x
     */
    public void userEntersValueTest(int x)
    {
        System.out.println("User enters x: " + x);
        this.x = x;
    }
}
```

A more traditional alternative would be a documentation driven approach to system level testing. A set of tests is devised that have a broad scope intended to demonstrate whether the software is "fit for purpose". It is down to the developer to define that scope. Each test then specifies:

- The nature of the test.
- What data inputs are required.
- What data outputs or other side outputs are expected.
- What data output or other side outputs actually occurred when the test was performed.
- Whether the application has passed or failed this test.
- If the test is failed, what remedial action is required to address the problem.

In commercial software engineering, these tests are recorded using a structured test schedule document that might look like this:

Application/version		Tested by			Date	
Test ref	Description	Inputs	Expected outputs	Actual outputs	Pass/fail	If fail, action required
1	User enters invalid value for number of items required	10	"Invalid output"	Proceed to inventory	Fail	Check boundary conditions
2	User enters valid value for number if items required	1	Proceed to inventory	Proceed to inventory	Pass	–
...	...	...	...		...	...

The software is declared "fit for purpose" when it can pass all of the system level tests. If any test is failed, appropriate remedial action is taken (generally reworking some code) and the whole schedule is then carried out again. It is important to consider performing all of tests again as we cannot guarantee that any remedial coding has not affected the codebase such that one of the other tests would now fail. The system level testing documentation is then shipped with the application as proof of fitness for purpose.

6.6   The Basics of Exception Handling

Although we take every effort to eliminate errors in our code, it is unlikely that we can ever develop a completely error free codebase. So to have a robust application, we also have to have strategies to deal with issues that only arise when the program is running. We call these "run time" errors. Run time errors can occur because of poor coding, or because of problems interacting with user or external data content. Such errors lead to the "throwing of exceptions".

An **exception** is a situation when the program behaves in an unexpected manner usually indicating an error condition.

We say that the program "**throws an exception**".

Exceptions can be "**caught**" at code level as a way of trying to deal with the cause of the exception.

If an exception remains uncaught, the program will terminate with an "**uncaught exception error**".

A common example of an exception you might see the JVM throw would be a NullPointerException. Consider this code:

```
import java.util.*;

public class ExceptionExample1
{
    private ArrayList<String> myList;

    public void problemCode(String item)
    {
        myList.add(item);
    }
}
```

The code compiles fine. However, if we call problemCode(), we get a message from the JVM:

```
java.lang.NullPointerException
        at ExceptionExample1.problemCode(ExceptionExample1.java:15)
```

The problem here is that we declared myList, but forgot to initialise the object using the new operator. We then tried to perform a method call on a non-existent object. The JVM Is unable to comply and has thus raised an "exception" – a NullPointerException. There is no code to deal with this situation, so the program comes to a stop.

Java offers quite complex features to allow exceptions to be managed. As well as built in exceptions such as NullPointerException, we can also define our own exception building on the Java Exception class. We can then then "try" to execute a block of code, and raise an exception if an error condition arises. We can then create code that tries to "catch" these exceptions to see if the problem can be solved. If the exception remains uncaught, the program will stop. The following code example shows how we can use the idea of "try and catch":

```java
public void catchingAnException(String item)
{
    try
    {
        myList.add(item);
    }
    catch(NullPointerException e)
    {
        System.out.println("Problem!");
        myList = new ArrayList<String>();
        System.out.println("Now try again");
    }
}
```

In reality, this is poor coding as we should really have fixed the lack of initialisation in the first instance. But it does illustrate the broad code approach. The `try` block is executed, but a `NullPointerExcepption` is thrown on first execution. The code then looks around to see if the exception is caught. The JVM identifies that it is, and control transfers to the `catch` block. The method then completes and control passes back to the code that called the method in the first place.

A method can opt to catch as many different types of exception as required. We can also add a `finally` block to `try` and `catch`, The `finally` block provides for code that will be executed when a `return` statement is encountered during the processing of an exception.

We can define our own exceptions as well. All exceptions are sub classes of the Java `Throwable` class. Here is an extract of the hierarchy of `Throwable` classes:

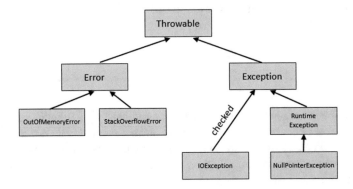

The Error sub class is concerned with low-level JVM issues. There is typically little we can do to fix these problems. The `Exception` sub class is then further sub classes into `RunTimeException`, and a set of "checked" exceptions such as `IOException`.

Checked exceptions are checked at compile time. If some code within a method can throw a checked exception, then the method must either handle the exception or it must specify the exception using the `throws` keyword. This is because some library classes need to be able to throw certain exceptions. For example a

BufferedReader object is used to open a file for reading. There may be an issue opening the file, and the BufferedReader object will throw an IOException in that case. So any method that utilises a BufferedReader has an obligation to either deal with the IOException itself, or be declared as throwing the exception so that it may be caught elsewhere. So the compiler demands that a clear undertaking is given by methods for checked exceptions.

```java
import java.io.*;

public class ExceptionExample2
{
    /**
     * Here we deal with the IOExeception locally.
     */
    public void openFileAndReadLinesV1()
    {
        try
        {
            FileReader f = new FileReader("C:\\test.txt");
            BufferedReader r = new BufferedReader(f);

            String line;
            line = r.readLine();
            while (line != null)
            {
                System.out.println(line);
                line = r.readLine();
            }
            r.close();
            f.close();
        }
        catch (IOException e)
        {
            System.out.println("Problem opening file");
        }
    }

    /**
     * Here we rely on something else to catch our exception.
     */
    public void openFileAndReadLinesV2() throws IOException
    {
        FileReader f = new FileReader("C:\\test.txt");
        BufferedReader r = new BufferedReader(f);

        String line;
        line = r.readLine();
        while (line != null)
        {
            System.out.println(line);
            line = r.readLine();
        }
        r.close();
        f.close();
    }
}
```

We can catch either a general exception, or a specific one. We could opt to catch
NullPointerException, or the broader set represented by Exception. We
can also define our own exceptions by sub classing Exception. For example,
let's say that we want to stop someone from adding blank content to an Array-
List of String:

```java
import java.util.*;

public class ExceptionExample3
{
    private ArrayList<String> allNotes;

    public ExceptionExample3()
    {
        allNotes = new ArrayList<String>();
    }

    public void addNote(String note)
    {
        try
        {
            if (note.trim().compareTo("")==0)
            {
                throw new BlankNoteException("blank note");
            }
            else
            {
                allNotes.add(note);
            }
        }
        catch (BlankNoteException e)
        {
            System.out.println("Try again!");
        }
    }
}

/**
 * To be thrown when blank notes are input
 *
 * @author Kingsley Sage
 * @version 1.0
 */

public class BlankNoteException extends Exception
{
    // Constructor
    public BlankNoteException(String message)
    {
        super(message);
    }
}
```

The `BlankNoteException` is its own class and extends `Exception`. It does not do very much, but does call the constructor in its parent class to display a message on the screen. That might not initially seem useful, but that same exception can be called elsewhere in the codebase, and thus can provide a useful and centralised means of dealing with errors. It is up to us to determine what useful code or actions the actual exception handling code will perform.

6.7   More Advanced Exception Handling

On first encounter, exception handling seems to be an idea that could have just as easily been achieved using some well-chosen `if` statements, and some problem solving methods. Whilst that is true, the real power of exception handling only becomes apparent when dealing with larger programs. Checking for errors, particularly in respect of user input, can be tedious and can obscure more important underlying code structures. Sometimes an error can occur deal in a chain or call stack of method calls. Rather than have lots of distributed error checking code, we can centralise the management of errors and then provide a single exception handler to deal with them. Consider the following call stack:

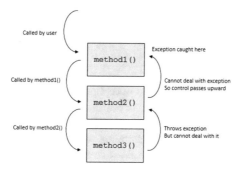

Here, `method1()` has invoked `method2()` which in turn has involved `method3()` to do some job. During execution, `method3()` hits a problem and throws an exception. The JVM refers to the call stack. Working up the call stack, the JVM determines that `method2()` is unable to help. But then the JVM locates an appropriate catch clause in `method1()`, so control is transferred there. Any method down the call stack could have thrown the exception and `method1()` would have been guaranteed to have caught it. Here is a code example to illustrate the example:

```
public class ExceptionExample4
{
    public void method1()
    {
        try
        {
            method2();
        }
        catch (ArithmeticException e)
        {
            System.out.println("method1() catches the error");
        }
    }

    public void method2()
    {
        method3();
    }

    public void method3() throws ArithmeticException
    {
        int x=0;
        // Does some useful work ...
        // But throws a built in ArithmeticException.
        // Note we do not need the try catch block here.
        if (x == 0)
        {
            throw new ArithmeticException("0 value");
        }
    }
}
```

In this case it is one of the built-in exceptions, the ArithmeticException that is thrown by method3(). However method3() lacks the means to deal with the ArithmeticException. Note that method3() does not need a try catch block. The method implementation simply notes that it can throw an ArithmeticException and then does so if needed. It's the catch block in method1() where the exception is actually dealt with.

In reality, the exception could have been caught in a different class a long way in code terms from the point where the exception was first thrown. So we can centralise the processing of errors rather than having lots of distributed error handling code throughout the codebase.

This is just an overview of the value of exception handling. As we have discussed in this chapter, error handling is a broad and complex topic, but essential in creating robust applications. There is no single one methodology for creating robust code, and creating such good code is not only good code craft, but a key element of the more over-arching philosophy of software engineering.

Deeper into Arrays and Collections

7

In Chap. 4, we met the versatile `ArrayList` class and saw that it could be used to represent a collection of any Java type. In this chapter we delve deeper into the world of arrays and collections, and some of the algorithms that can support us in using them.

7.1 Fixed Length Versus Dynamic Length Arrays

We defined the `ArrayList` as a class to store a collection of some single type. That collection can then have a dynamic size as we add objects to, and delete from, the `ArrayList` at run time. We have seen that the wrapper classes serve to allow the primitive types to act as if they were objects. But is such flexibility always to our advantage, and is there is a simpler way of dealing with groups of primitive data?

Recall that the purpose of OO is to allow us to model some real-world problem in a useful manner. Sometimes we have a group of things, and we know precisely how big that group will be, and also that the size will never change. A good example might be the set of numbers of a lottery ticket. Such a ticket might have 6 `int` numbers. Every ticket always has 6 numbers with no exceptions. So a flexible length arrangement to store the numbers on a ticket seems overkill. In fact, it also poses a possible source of error, since it would be possible at the code level to add too many numbers to the ticket. So in OO design terms, whenever we have grouped data, we should consider whether it needs to be flexible or fixed length.

> If some grouped data in the problem domain has **a fixed size or length**, then we should use a fixed size representation such as an **array**. Fixed length arrays may consist of primitive data or objects.

© Springer Nature Switzerland AG 2019
K. Sage, *Concise Guide to Object-Oriented Programming*,
Undergraduate Topics in Computer Science,
https://doi.org/10.1007/978-3-030-13304-7_7

If some grouped data in the problem data has an **unknown size or length**, or
it can change during the course of the program, then we should use a dynamic
size **Collection type** such as an `ArrayList`. Collections must be of object
types. Primitive types must be wrapped to participate in collections.

Fixed length arrays are not classes, and so do not have methods. However, as we
shall see later, there is a static utility class `Arrays` that provides some useful
algorithms for working with arrays (notably for searching and sorting). Note that we
should not refer to fixed length arrays as Collections, as the latter term is a
framework for dynamic length class based groupings such as `ArrayList`.

Historically there are some other advantages in using fixed length arrays in that
the amount of memory they occupy can be pre-computed, allowing the run time
environment to reserve and organise memory in an efficient manner. However, this
difference is somewhat moot in Java as organisation of memory within the JVM is
hidden from the user by design, although there can be some running time performance issues that are optimised by using fixed length arrays.

7.2 Fixed Length Arrays of Primitive Types

A fixed length array has the advantage that we can store arrays of primitive data
without needing to resort to wrappers. All we need to do is to declare and initialise
the array and then use it. For example, let's create a `LotteryTicket` class for
our own lottery where each ticket has 6 `int` numbers in the range 1–99 inclusive:

```
import java.util.*;


public class LotteryTicket
{
    // declare numbers as an array of type int
    private int[] numbers;

    public LotteryTicket()
    {
        // initialise the numbers array
        numbers = new int[6];
        Random r = new Random();
        for (int x=0; x < numbers.length; x++)
        {
            // Set each number in the range 1-99
            int num = r.nextInt(98)+1;
            numbers[x] = num;
        }
    }
}
```

To declare an array type, we add the square brackets [] after the type. We initialise the array using the new operator, but note that this does not mean the numbers is a Collection—it's an array. We then use a Random object to fill the array. Note that the array has a property length. Don't be tempted to think that length is a method—it lacks the brackets associated with methods. It just enables the compiler to look up the length of the array and makes it easier to maintain and updated code (we need only change one character if we wanted there to be 8 numbers on a ticket).

As an alternative, we can declare arrays and initialise with set values all in one go:

```
private int[] moreNumbers = {1,4,5,2,10};
```

To access an individual element of an array, we refer to it by the name of the array and then an int value for the index in square brackets:

Array elements are referred to using an index e.g. numbers[<*index*>].
An array index must be an int, and cannot be a negative number.
Array indices are zero referenced, so the first element is at index 0, e.g. numbers[0].
If an array has N elements, they are numbered contiguously from 0 to N-1.
Unaccessed elements will remain at the default value for the corresponding primitive type.
An attempt to access elements outside of the permitted range will cause an ArrayIndexOutOfBoundsException to be thrown.

If we instantiate the LotteryTicket class, we can use the BlueJ inspector to see our array:

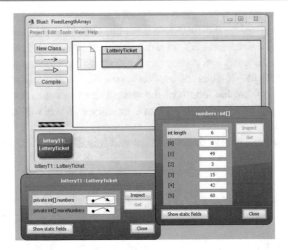

We can now add a method to display our ticket numbers:

```
public void displayNumbers()
{
    System.out.println("The numbers are: ");
    for (int x=0; x<numbers.length; x++)
    {
        System.out.print(numbers[x] + " ");
    }
    System.out.println("Good luck!");
}
```

NB: `System.out.print()` simply omits the new line/carriage return when displaying data.

7.3   Fixed Length Arrays of Objects

Although it is tempting to regard arrays as just suited to primitive types, and collections as suited to objects, we can also create fixed length arrays of object types, and for the same reasons of "if you know the size is fixed, make it fixed". Let's say we wanted to build a fixed length array of `String`:

```
public class SmallDictionary
{
    private String[] myWords;

    public SmallDictionary()
    {
        myWords = new String[10];
        myWords[0] = "crocodile";
        myWords[1] = "zebra";
        myWords[2] = "gnu";
        myWords[9] = new String("parrot");
    }

    public void displayWords()
    {
        for (int x=0; x < myWords.length; x++)
        {
            System.out.println(myWords[x]);
        }
    }
}
```

We see that we create the array `myWords` as before. But this time the array elements are instances of type `String`. Remember "parrot" is just a syntactic shorthand for `new String("parrot")`. Note here that we only filled four of the elements. The remaining elements in `myWords` will remain `null` until objects are created and placed in them. `System.out.println()` will display `null` when we try to display the element as text on the screen.

We can create a fixed length array of any Java object type. As before, the array must be of a single type. If we inspect the array, we will see the characteristic curved arrow marking inviting us to click through the array inspection to see the underlying objects in that array.

7.4 Multi-dimensional Arrays

As well as simple linear one-dimensional fixed length arrays, we can also extend to multiple dimensions—typically two or three. Two dimensional arrays are useful for grid style representation (e.g. a TicTacToe board) or image data. Three dimensional arrays may find applications in CAD and physical world modelling. Higher order dimension arrays are possible, but their uses would be more narrow, and they have the potential to be memory intensive.

A two-dimensional array can be regarded as organised into rows and columns, like a matrix or a spreadsheet. We address a two-dimensional array by row first, the column. It is also necessary when declaring an array to specify the at least size of the leading dimension (i.e. row) so that the compiler may perform array memory access in an appropriate manner. For rectangular arrays, it is common to specify the size of both the rows and columns. The following example is the start of a simple TicTacToe board, using a 3 × 3 array of primitive type char:

```java
public class TicTacToeBoard
{
    private char[][] board;

    public TicTacToeBoard()
    {
        board = new char[3][3];
        for (int row=0; row<board.length; row++)
        {
            for (int col=0; col<board[row].length; col++)
            {
                board[row][col] = '-';
            }
        }
    }

    public void fillSpaceOnBoard(int row, int col, char value)
    {
        if ((row < board.length)&&(col < board[row].length))
        {
            board[row][col] = value;
        }
    }

    public void displayBoard()
    {
        for (int row=0; row < board.length; row++)
        {
            for (int col=0; col < board[row].length; col++)
            {
                System.out.print(board[row][col] + " ");
            }
            System.out.println();
        }
    }

    public void makeSomeMoves()
    {
        fillSpaceOnBoard(1,1,'X');
        fillSpaceOnBoard(0,2,'O');
        displayBoard();
    }
}
```

When we call the makeSomeMoves() method we get:

```
- - O
- X -
- - -
```

Note the extended use of the `length` property. If we use `length` on its own we are referring to the size of the first dimension (the number of rows in this case). If we want to find the number of columns for a specific row we first select the row and then apply the `length` property e.g. `board[1].length` is the number of columns associated with row 1. This implies that, as well as rectangular arrays, we can have jagged arrays where the number of columns for each row is different. That could use useful for a simple dictionary class, where the words are stored in an array where each row corresponds to an initial letter of the alphabet. In this example the number of words in each row can vary:

```
public class BetterDictionary
{
    private String[][] allWords;

    public BetterDictionary()
    {
        // Note we do not specify the second dimension size
        allWords = new String[26][];

        // We can setup our Strings in a number of ways ..
        String[] aWords = {"aardvark","act","apple","azure"};
        allWords[0] = aWords;
        String[] bWords = {"bake","banana","byte"};
        allWords[1] = bWords;
        allWords[2] = new String[2];
        allWords[2][0] = "cat";
        allWords[2][1] = new String("crayon");
    }

    /**
     * Display words starting with letter at row
     * position c.
     * @param int c where a=0, b=1 and so on.
     */
    public void displayWordsForLetter(int c)
    {
        System.out.println("Words for letter " + c);
        for (int x=0; x<allWords[c].length;x++)
        {
            System.out.print(allWords[c][x] + " ");
        }
    }
}
```

In fact this two-dimensional array is an "array of arrays" and this explains why we can have either rectangular or jagged array constructions.

If we use the BlueJ inspector, we see the ragged nature of the array storage:

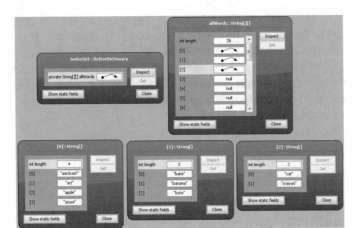

Of course, no self-respecting dictionary or collection of numbers would be useful if it could not be sorted.

7.5   Sorting Data

Sorting is one of the most basic operations that we perform on data in computer science. Whether we are sorting spreadsheet data in date order, or value, or organising a dictionary into alphabetic order to facilitate efficient search, sorting is a key aspect of data management. There is a whole branch of algorithms in computer science dedicated to sorting data. So it should not surprise you that Java comes with a variety of sorting algorithms in its libraries.

We don't concern ourselves with how the sorting process takes place. All we need is the API and a notion of what constitutes the order we want to search according to. Where sensible, Java applies a default notion of "natural order", for example arrays of int are sorted into ascending order, and String by alphanumeric order. As we shall see later, sometimes we need to provide a little help.

For arrays of primate types, we turn to the static utility library Arrays. Recall that utility libraries contain only static methods and do no need to be instantiated; there are only ever one of them. Revising our LotteryTicket example from the previous section, we can sort our random numbers as simply as calling Arrays.sort() The sort is performed "in situ" so no additional data structures are required:

```
        // Sort the numbers into their natural
        // ascending order ...
        Arrays.sort(numbers);
```

We can similarly sort the one-dimensional dictionary. Note that we cannot leave any element of the array of `String` as null, or the sorting algorithm will throw a `NullPointerException`:

```
        myWords = new String[10];
        myWords[0] = "crocodile";
        myWords[1] = "zebra";
        myWords[2] = "gnu";
        myWords[3] = "ball";
        myWords[4] = "cup";
        myWords[5] = "hovercraft";
        myWords[6] = "telescope";
        myWords[7] = "xylophone";
        myWords[8] = "aardvark";
        myWords[9] = new String("parrot");

        // Sort the small dictionary
        Arrays.sort(myWords);
```

In the case of an array of `String`, the natural order is forwards alphanumeric. The `Arrays` class also has provision for alternative orderings, such as reverse order:

```
    public void reverseSort()
    {
        Arrays.sort(myWords,Collections.reverseOrder());
        displayWords();
    }
```

We cannot specify alternative orderings for arrays of primitive types. The custom ordering of arrays of objects is achieved using a `static` method from the `Collections` class. This in turn masks the use of a `Comparator` class.

So we can sort fixed length arrays, but what about collections? For something like an `ArrayList` of `String`, it's very much the same concept, except that an `ArrayList` is a Java `Collection` type, and so we use the `Collections` utility methods to sort instead:

```
import java.util.*;

public class DynamicDictionary
{
    private ArrayList<String> allWords;

    public DynamicDictionary()
    {
        allWords = new ArrayList<String>();
        allWords.add("crocodile");
        allWords.add("zither");
        allWords.add("cake");
        allWords.add("xylophone");
        allWords.add("cat");
        allWords.add("flower");
        allWords.add("forest");
    }

    public void listWords()
    {
        for (String w:allWords)
        {
            System.out.println(w);
        }
    }

    public void sortWords()
    {
        Collections.sort(allWords);
    }
}
```

For an `ArrayList` of `String`, there is a clear natural order. This is true for other `ArrayList` collections, including collections of wrapped types. But what about situations where:

- We want an alternative ordering, such as reverse number order, or reverse alphanumeric?
- We have a `Collection` of a type with no obvious natural order, or a class that we created where there are many ways that ordering could occur?

In this case we have to provide the `Collections.sort()` method with some help. This help can be implemented by using the `Comparator` and `Comparable` interfaces:

A class can implement the `Comparable` interface. The interface requires a concrete implementation of the `compareTo()` method. This provides the basis for the default natural order for a collection of that class type.

An additional support class can be created that implements the `Comparator` interface. This interface requires a concrete implementation of the `compare()` method. The additional class then then be supplied to the `Collections.sort()` method to facilitate sorting of a collection of a class. Many different support classes can be created to permit a range of different sort orderings to be used.

As a general rule, `Comparable` is suited when there is only one default ordering, and `Comparator` where there may be different orderings needed at different times.

Once Java can establish how to compare two instances of a class, it can use a general search algorithm to sort an entire collection. So the `compareTo()` and `compare()` methods just need to compare two instances. They work in slightly different ways:

The `compareTo()` method compares an instance of a current object to another instance provided as an argument, and returns a negative integer, zero, or a positive integer if the current object is less than, equal to or greater than the argument object.

The `compare()` method compare two instances of a class as arguments and returns a negative integer, zero, or a positive integer if the first argument is less than, equal to or greater than the second argument.

Let's start by building a class to represent antique artefacts that just needs a single natural ordering. As such it implements the `Comparable` interface. The interface requires providing the implementation of the `compareTo()` method and then we can use `Collections.sort()` to do the actual sorting:

```
public class Antique implements Comparable<Antique>
{
    private String name;
    private double value;
    private int yearCreated;

    public Antique(String name,double value, int yearCreated)
    {
        this.name = name;
        this.value = value;
        this.yearCreated = yearCreated;
    }

    // Needed to allow Collections.sort to access value
    public double getValue()
    {
        return value;
    }
    public String getName()
    {
        return name;
    }
    public int getYearCreated()
    {
        return yearCreated;
    }

    // To complete the Comparable interface
    public int compareTo(Antique x)
    {
        if (value == x.getValue())
        {
            return 0;
        }
        else if (value < x.getValue())
        {
            return -1;
        }
        else
        {
            return +1;
        }
    }

    public void showDetails()
    {
        System.out.println(name + ", worth £" +
            String.format("%.2f",value) + " pounds");
    }
}
```

We can now create an `AntiqueShop` that manages a collection of `Antique`:

```java
import java.util.*;

public class AntiqueShop
{
    private ArrayList<Antique> allAntiques;

    public AntiqueShop()
    {
        allAntiques = new ArrayList<Antique>();
        allAntiques.add(new Antique("ming vase",5000,1400));
        allAntiques.add(new Antique("painting1",10000,1950));
        allAntiques.add(new Antique("harrison watch",8000,1750));
        allAntiques.add(new Antique("sketchbook",200,1978));
    }

    public void showAllAntiques()
    {
        for (Antique a:allAntiques)
        {
            a.showDetails();
        }
    }

    public void sortAntiques()
    {
        Collections.sort(allAntiques);
    }
}
```

If we instantiate the `AntiqueShop` and `showAllAntiques()`, the elements are in the order they were added to the linear `ArrayList`. Now we call `sortAntiques()` and then `showAllAntiques()` again and we find the elements are now in order of increasing value. Note that the `compareTo()` method in `Antique` will need to provide an accessor for the variable used for the sorting as the factor ay method `compareTo()` is fetching a value from an external instance of the same class.

As a bonus, the `Collections.sort ()` factory method can now also perform a reverse order. The `reverseSortAntiques()` method does exactly that.

As an alternative to a single natural ordering, we can use the `Comparator` interface to make many orderings. We will continue to use our `Antique` example. We want to be able to sort the antiques by `yearCreated` in ascending order. So we create a new class `YearCreatedComaparator` that implements the `Comparator` interface:

```
import java.util.*;

public class YearCreatedComparator implements Comparator<Antique>
{
    // To complete the Comparator interface
    public int compare(Antique a1, Antique a2)
    {
        if (a1.getYearCreated() == a2.getYearCreated())
        {
            return 0;
        }
        else if (a1.getYearCreated() < a2.getYearCreated())
        {
            return -1;
        }
        else
        {
            return +1;
        }
    }
}
```

Now when we invoke Collections.sort(), we instantiate an instance of YearCreatedComparator and pass it as an argument. We can add this to our AntiqueShop class:

```
public void sortByAgeCreated()
{
    Collections.sort(allAntiques, new YearCreatedComparator());
}
```

We can now create as many new comparison classes as we wish. When we sort, we provide an instance of that class and that directs the Collections.sort() method.

We do not have to choose exclusively between these two approaches. Out Antique class has both a natural default order, and we can create additional Comparator classes and specify the sort order of our choosing. This is a very flexible means of sorting any ArrayList collections.

7.6   Hash Functions

Up to now, we have considered linear array and collections. By linear we simply mean that they are stored "in a line" with elements starting at position 0, and with elements occupying contiguously numbered index positions. When we add elements to an ArrayList, the elements are added in increasing index order, although we can subsequently re-order them as we saw in the previous section. If we remove an element from an `ArrayList`, then the elements after the one we removed move up to ensure that the numbering scheme remains contiguous. This provides a very understandable linear storage. It only really has one disadvantage and that relates to search. If we wish to find an element in a linear list, we have to search the list one element at a time to find it. The ordering can certainly help, but ultimately as the list grows in length, the time it takes to search for a specific element will increase. For simpler linear list search, we note that the complexity class of the search operation is upper bounded by $O(n)$ where n is the number of elements in the list.

For really large collections, this can pose performance issues. So as an alternative, we can consider a different means of organising and searching a collection based on the concept of a "hash table".

A **hash table** is a means of organising a collection of elements such that they can be sorted in approximately **constant time**. This means that the time to locate an element is about the same regardless of the number of elements in the collection.

Hash tables rely on the notion of a hash function. A hash function is a mathematical formula that you apply to some data that produces an integer number. That integer number suggests where the data element should be stored. For example, imagine the letters of the English alphabet are numbered 1 (for a) through to 26 (for z). One hash function would be just to add the letter values together. So the has function for the word "cat" would be 3 + 1 + 20 = 24. So we store the word in the 24th element of a collection. So if we want to see if "cat" is in our collection, compute the hash function and look in that space in the hash table. If the space is empty, the word was not there.

In reality, more than one word is likely to give the same has function value, so we need to add a few more rules. For another word with a hash function value of 24, we need to move along to position 25. This is called "linear probing". With a few more rules we can construct a process whereby we can quickly look up elements by their hash function value in almost a constant amount of time (the probing processes do add a bit of variation).

If the collection size is smaller than the largest value that the hash function can produce, we just take the remainder after division (modulo) when integer dividing the hash function by the length of the collection. So if "cat" has a hash function of 24, and the hash table has space for 10 elements, then 24 % 10 = 4 (there is a remainder of 4) and we store "cat" at position 4.

In reality the design of efficient hash function and probing strategies is a complex subject. But we do not have to concern ourselves with, as all Java objects come with one built in. The Java language base `Object` has a `public hashCode()` method and all objects inherit it from that class. We can see it in action:

```
s1 = "crocodile";
s2 = "teapot";
System.out.println(s1 + " " + s1.hashCode());
System.out.println(s2 + " " + s2.hashCode());
```

7.7 The HashMap Class

We can make use of the hash function as a means of affording almost constant time search, The Java HashMap class provides an effective implementation of this kind of storage. A HashMap is a Java collection that stores elements in the form of "key-value pairs".

A **key-value pair** is a 2-tuple data structure. The **key** is used to determine where in a hash table the **value** should be stored. The storage spaces in the hash table are frequently referred to as **buckets**.

Both the **key and the value must be object types** (as primitives lack a hashCode() method). The key and value can be different object types.

Keys must be unique. Probing is used to deal with situations where two keys used produce the same hash function value. **Values do not need to be unique**.

Values can be **looked up** in the hash table by **key**.

So a HashMap can be thought of as a type of "lookup directory":

Key (a String)	Value (a String)
"John Smith"	"Carpenter"
"Mario"	"Plumber"
"Shelia Hughes"	"Teacher"
"Fred Twist"	"Teacher"

HashMap is generic, so any object type can serve as the key and value, and they do not need to be the same. The HashMap offers a range of methods and some of the most useful are:

Method	Description
boolean put(K key, V value)	Adds an entry in the map with key K and value V
void clear()	Remover all elements from the collection
E get(Object key)	Retrieve element of type E for the specified key
boolean isEmpty()	Returns true if the collection is empty
V remove(Object key)	Removes the element specified by the key (returns the value V)
int size()	Returns the number of elements in the collection

To declare and initialise an instance of a HashMap:

```
import java.util.*;

<access-modifier> HashMap< <key-type> <value-type> > <field-name>

<field-name> = new HashMap< <key-type> <value-type> > ();
```

Here is a complete code example of a HashMap in action:

```
import java.util.*;

public class HashMapExample
{
    private HashMap<String, String> allRecords;

    public HashMapExample()
    {
        // The key is of type String.
        // The value is of type String.
        allRecords = new HashMap<String,String>();
        allRecords.put("John Smith","Carpenter");
        allRecords.put("Mario","Plumber");
        allRecords.put("Sheila Hughes","Teacher");
        allRecords.put("Fred Twist","Teacher");
    }
}
```

If we inspect the HashMap, we note that the elements are spread through the underlying hash table. It is important that the underlying table operates with some free space, to assist in solving the probing issue (a concept referred to as the "loading factor").

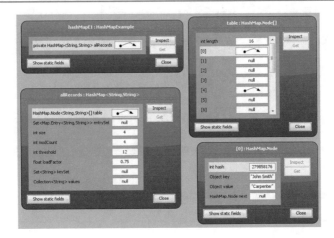

If we tried to add a new element to the HashMap with a duplicate key, it would not be added and the size of the collection would remain unchanged.

Now we can implement a method searchFor() that searches our collection for a given key value:

```
public boolean searchFor(String s)
    {
        String r = allRecords.get(s);
        if (r != null)
        {
            return true;
        }
        else
        {
            return false;
        }
    }
```

This is a simpler approach than iterating our way through a linear collection such as an ArrayList. The only downside is that our domain may have multiple mappings from a key to values. In a telephone directory, it's perfectly possible that there are two different people with the name "John Smith" and a HashMap cannot permit duplicate keys. One solution would be to concatenate the name with an address or other identifying data. But there are other situations where it is useful to have collections with guaranteed unique values.

7.8   The HashSet Class

The HashSet class is somewhat unhelpfully named in that it does not offer any key/value pairs like HashMap. Although the name might suggest they are closely related, they are quite different. It is worth summarising some terminology here.

> In maths and computer science:
>
> A **List** (such as an **ArrayList**) is a collection of elements where **order in unimportant** to the meaning of the Collection, and **duplicate elements can exist**.
>
> A **Map** (such as **HashMap**) is a collection of elements organised as **key/value pairs**, where the **key must be unique**.
>
> A **Set** (such as **HashSet**) is a collection of elements where **each element of the collection must be unique**.

The implementation of HashSet uses a hash table in its underlying implementation, but these details are abstracted away from us. The purpose of the HashSet is to provide a set collection where no duplicate object references exist. Note that this does not means that duplicate object internal values can't exist, as long as they are not actually the same object. A good example might be a pack of playing cards. There is only one of each card.

HashSet is generic, so it can serve as a set collection of any Java object type. The HashSet offers a range of methods and some of the most useful are:

Method	Description
boolean add(K e)	Adds object e to the set if not already present.
void clear()	Remover all elements from the set.
boolean contains(Object o)	Returns true if the object o is present in the collection.
boolean isEmpty()	Returns true if the collection is empty
boolean remove(Object o)	Removes the element from the set if it is present.
int size()	Returns the number of elements in the collection.

To declare and initialise an instance of a HashSet:

```
import java.util.*;

<access-modifier> HashSet< <object-type> > <field-name>

<field-name> = new HashSet< <object-type> > ();
```

Here is a complete code example of a `HashSet` in action modelling a pack of cards. We start with a `Card` class and then use a `HashSet` to store a set collection `HashSet` of type `Card`:

```java
public class Card
{
    private char value; // e.g. '1','2' .. 'Q','K'
    private String suit; // e.g. "Diamonds", "Spades"

    public Card(char value, String suit)
    {
        this.suit = suit;
        this.value = value;
    }
    public String getSuit()
    {
        return suit;
    }

    public char getValue()
    {
        return value;
    }
}
public class HashSetDemo
{
    private HashSet<Card> cardPack;
    public HashSetDemo()
    {
        // We happen to know there are at
        // most exactly 52 max cards.
        cardPack = new HashSet<Card>(52);
        Card c1 = new Card('A',"Spades");
        Card c2 = new Card('2',"Spades");
        Card c3 = new Card('3',"Spades");

        // Could just keep on adding cards ...
        cardPack.add(c1); // ignoring returned value
        cardPack.add(c2);
        cardPack.add(c3);

        // Now the size is 3
        showSize();

        // Now try to add c1 again ...
        cardPack.add(c1);

        // Size remains the same
        showSize();

        // But we can create another distinct object
        // with the same internal data ...
        Card c4 = new Card('A',"Spades");
        cardPack.add(c4);

        // Size is now 4 ...
        showSize();
    }
    public void showSize()
    {
        System.out.println("Number of elements: "
                            + cardPack.size());
    }
}
```

If we try to add c1 again, we would note that the add() method will return false and the size would remain three. But if we create a new Card c4, who also happens to be "an ace of spades" then we can add it successfully to the set as it is a distinct object. So we must exercise care to ensure that we understand the difference between two objects that are distinct instances, and two object references that refer to the same object in memory.

7.9 Iterating Through Collections

One of the most common tasks for working with any collection is the ability to iterate through the elements. We have already seen that for an ArrayList this can be done conveniently using a for loop. Iterating through our collections such as HashMap and HashSet is a little less straightforward. But for many OO applications, we would like to have common patterns or means of iterating through any collection type. Such a pattern is realised in Java using the Iterator interface. Each collection type has an iterator() method that return an instance of an Iterator that in turn provides methods to facilitate iterating through the collection.

The two key methods defined by the Iterator interface are:

Method	Description
boolean hasNext()	Returns true if there are more elements in the collection
E next()	Returns an object E that is the next object iterating through the collection

We can now examine three different ways of iterating through an ArrayList. Two using loops, and one using an Iterator:

```
import java.util.*;

public class IterationExample
{
    private ArrayList<String> myList;
    private HashMap<String,String> myMap; // used later
    private HashSet<String> mySet;        // used later

    public IterationExample()
    {
        myList = new ArrayList<String>();
        myMap = new HashMap<String,String>(); // used later
        mySet = new HashSet<String>();         // used later
    }

    public void listExample()
    {
        myList.add("egg");
        myList.add("potato");
        myList.add("beans");

        // Using a for loop
        for (int i=0; i<myLisL.size(); i++)
        {
            System.out.println(myList.get(i));
        }

        // Using a for each style loop
        for (String s:myList)
        {
            System.out.println(s);
        }

        // Using an iterator
        Iterator it = myList.iterator();
        while (it.hasNext())
        {
            String s = (String) it.next();
            System.out.println(s);
        }
    }
}
```

In the `Iterator` example, note the use of the explicit cast in the call to `next()`. This is because `next()` is declared as returning an `Object`, but we know in reality that object is a `String`.

Using a `for` loop for a `HashMap` would be more complex. Instead we have two options:

- Get a set of keys and then iterate through each key to recover the corresponding values.
- Get a set of key/value pairings (called a `Map.Entry` pairing).

Both can be achieved conveniently using an `Iterator`:

```java
public void mapExample()
{
    myMap.put("John Smith","pilot");
    myMap.put("Jenny Howell","artist");
    myMap.put("Neville Jones","writer");

    // Using an iterator - fetching pairs
    Iterator it1 = myMap.entrySet().iterator();
    while (it1.hasNext())
    {
        Map.Entry pair = (Map.Entry) it1.next();
        String k = (String) pair.getKey();
        String v = (String) pair.getValue();
        System.out.println(k + ", " + v);
    }

    // Using an iterator over the keySet()
    Iterator it2 = myMap.keySet().iterator();
    while (it2.hasNext())
    {
        String k = (String) it2.next();
        String v = myMap.get(k);
        System.out.println(k + ", " + v);
    }
}
```

We can also use the `Iterator` with the `HashSet`:

```java
public void setExample()
{
    mySet.add("Kirk");
    mySet.add("Spock");
    mySet.add("Scotty");

    // Using an iterator
    Iterator it = mySet.iterator();
    while (it.hasNext())
    {
        String s = (String) it.next();
        System.out.println(s);
    }
}
```

You can use an `Iterator` with all Java collection types. This provides a simple and common style pattern for iterating through a collection and helps to standardise our coding style and make the codebase more consistent and readable.

There are many other Java collection types for you to explore. But `ArrayList`, `HashMap` and `HashSet` are arguably the most commonplace. The use of the others would require a more thorough discussion of computer science data structures and algorithms, and that is beyond the scope of this book. At this stage, we simply need to consider the broad purpose of lists, maps and sets, and choose them as the right solution for any real-world problem domain we are modelling.

Adding a Graphical User Interface

8

Up to now, we have built Java programs with solely text-based interfaces relying on features contained within BlueJ to create key objects and to call methods. Whilst this has helped us to develop our understanding of the Java language and the principles of programming, it is not how most applications are used in the real world. Solely text-based applications are far and few in number, generally confined to console applications for fine grained operating system activities and batch files. The world, now rich in processing power, smartphones, tablets and desktop-based OS technology, has moved to applications controlled by ever more sophisticated Graphical User Interfaces (GUIs). So no book on Java or programming could really claim to be rounded unless it looked at the practice and development of a GUI.

It should be noted however that GUI design and implementation is a major undertaking in its own right. On the one hand, GUI design need to address Human Computer Interaction (HCI) issues such as usability and accessibility. This is complex subject rooted in psychology and a major area of study. On the other hand, GUI design has a range of technology issues such as the ease with which a GUI can be adapted independently of the underlying application, how it can be customised to appear differently on multiple platforms, and the libraries and frameworks that are needed to support it. Different languages offer a wide range of proprietary and open source code libraries for GUI development, each with their own particular needs and advantages and there is nowhere near the same degree of standardisation and consensus as to which approach is best.

One of the key underlying aims of the Java language was to provide a platform neutral language delivered through a virtual machine. This presents its own challenges as it implies that any GUI technology for use with Java must also be platform neutral. But the range of hardware that the virtual machines may be running on physically may vary enormously, each with their own particular limitations or specific adaptations in graphical and other UI capability. So any GUI libraries for Java must necessarily be designed in a manner relatively neutral to any particular technology, and instead focus on a more generalised view of what constitutes a GUI and how it may be delivered.

© Springer Nature Switzerland AG 2019
K. Sage, *Concise Guide to Object-Oriented Programming*,
Undergraduate Topics in Computer Science,
https://doi.org/10.1007/978-3-030-13304-7_8

In this chapter we need to investigate two broad themes:

- What general strategies can we adopt to help us build a GUI. HCI issues are beyond the scope of this book and we will instead focus on this idea in the context of the software code level design.
- The actual libraries and capabilities within Java that we can use to implement a GUI.

We focus on the Swing Java libraries for this second theme. Although there are other libraries, Swing is the most established and forms a part of all Java development toolkits. We will look at the basic concepts needed to build a useful Swing application, and build it as a fully usable standalone application.

Note that Swing and GUI design is a very significant subject, and easily commands a text book in its own right. As such, this book can only ever hope to serve as a broad introduction to the topic, supported with some small-scale examples to guide the reader into understanding the principles, and equip them with enough knowledge to engage with the huge range of materials available elsewhere and further their practical development skills and experience.

8.1   The Model View Controller MVC Design Pattern

Before we get into the code details of the Swing library, we first need to consider broader architectural ideas that will shape out ideas of how to develop a GUI, and the relationship that the GUI will have with its underlying application codebase. There are many drivers that will shape our thinking. Any significant application is likely to have a team working on it. That team will likely consist of specialists in different areas. Some may be algorithm developers, some generalist coders, some specialists in data management, and some specialists in GUI design and implementation. They may all be producing code that needs to be integrated to build a final working application. As with any project undertaking, the success of such a team-based development depends on the ability of the team to work together effectively. The requirements of a modern software project may also be driven by need for flexibility, implementation over a range of highly diverse devices e.g. tablet, mobile, desktop and on-line, with an emphasis on achieving functionality at the lowest possible development cost and on short timescales. All these factors influence the lifecycle processes through which modern software is developed.

One way that the development process itself can help us deliver on all of these challenges is to adopt designs that promote software re-use (a key ambition of OO design in any case) and that promote a modular approach to development. Consider the following example:

Company X develops code in response to a customer requirement for a desktop application with a GUI. The company delivers the codebase, but then gets a request for a similarly functional application but with a GUI for use on mobile device.

There are two possible ways that the scenario could play out:

- The GUI design is highly integrated into the underlying application codebase, so changing the GUI would require a substantial rebuild of the entire application from the ground up.
- The GUI is actually an independent element of the application codebase, with a strong separation of the code that constitutes the GUI from the underlying code base. Although the GUI will need to be redeveloped for the new device, the underlying codebase will remain essentially unchanged and so this rework can be delivered at a substantially lower cost than the original project.

This second scenario is highly desirable, but it requires a decision upfront at the application design stage. The notion that the GUI should be, to the extent that is practicable, separated from the underlying application code, is a very valuable design idea:

- The GUI code and the application (or business logic) code are likely to be the responsibilities of separate development teams in larger projects.
- It should be possible to redevelop the GUI element without making substantive changes to the underling application code base. This permits the same application to be presented ("skinned") in many different ways, possibly dependent on the run time environment (in the same vein that modern websites deliver content dependent on the calling device).
- Changes to the GUI can be made without affecting the correctness or validity of the underling application.
- Re-use of the application code base is possible, and the broad OO design principles of encapsulation and cohesion are promoted.

Modern software engineering also promotes the concept of "design patterns".

A **design pattern** is a template for solving a recurring problem. It represents a widely regarded way of achieving a useful solution, resulting typically from years of collective experience of trying to solve that problem.

A design pattern is neither a code solution, nor tied to any particular development language. Rather it represents an abstract strategy or set of principles. The same design pattern can be deployed in multiple languages.

A design pattern provides a **common terminology** for describing a problem.

Design patterns are a broad concept with applicability beyond the world of software engineering. For example, modern cars share a common design pattern in terms of the function and layout of their controls (such as the pedals and instruments), not shared by cars from the early 20th century when manufacturers adopted their own conventions and standards. Software design patterns are intended to help us construct applications in a way that are likely to be understood widely. There are many such patterns in common and it is an extensive subject in its own right. But for the development of a GUI, there is one architectural design pattern that we shall focus on; the "Model View Controller" (MVC) pattern.

The MVC pattern supports the notion of the "separation of concerns" and "responsibility driven design". As a pattern, it separates the architecture of an application into three parts:

- **Model**: The underlying application or business logic that is concerned solely with how the application operates, with no regard for its physical presentation or how the user interacts with it.
- **View**: The physical presentation (i.e. the appearance of the user interface) that is concerned solely with presentation, and not how the underlying application logic functions. The View may be updated by the Model.
- **Controller**: The part of the interface concerned with user interaction. Such interaction may take the form of buttons, sliders, touch, gesture, voice input and so on—whatever forms of interaction that are required to allow the user to communicate with the application.

The complete application then requires these three elements to work together:

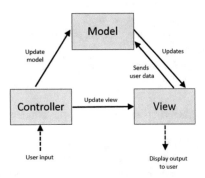

The Model maintains all underlying data and provides the core application functionality. Public data from that underlying application is rendered by the View. The Controller accepts user input and uses it to change the View (e.g. look at a particular aspect, page, menu or sub menu), and to send requests to the Model for operations to be performed.

If we adopt this design pattern, it should be possible to minimise the coupling between these elements to just those interaction that are required to make the application work. If we chose to change one of the elements e.g. redesign the appearance of the GUI, it should be possible to achieve this with minimal impact on the other architectural elements. Note that, in common with all design patterns, this is an aspiration and not a straitjacket. The extent that we pursue the pattern is down to us.

In coding terms, many Java applications are built this way. Swing embraces this design pattern, but many smaller Swing applications will tend to combine aspects of the View and Controller together. There is nothing particularly wrong with that—it just depends on what broader goals we have for further incremental software engineering development. In our examples, we will pursue a design pattern with a distinct Model on the one part, a hybrid View and Controller on the other part.

Now what we have laid the ground in terms of our software engineering objectives, it's time to start looking at the specifics of the Swing library.

8.2   Introducing Swing and AWT

Swing is best described as a GUI widget toolkit for the Java language, although it is often just described as a library. It forms part of the Java Foundation Classes i.e. it is a part of the regular Java landscape rather than a bolt on and its purpose is to provide a means of delivering GUIs for Java programs. Swing is in turn built on top of an earlier generation GUI toolkit the Abstract Window Toolkit (AWT).

The Swing library classes are written in Java so that they are platform independent and these classes, along with all other Java classes, are fully documented in the on-line documentation maintained by Oracle. The Swing classes are intended to be highly customisable and users can take existing Swing classes and augment their behaviour by sub classing them and/or by overriding default method implementations. Although it may seem bewildering at first, Swing is intended as a lightweight library and embraces the MVC design pattern. The term "lightweight" here generally refers to the notion that is does not require direct interaction with the host operating systems resources (as the Swing classes are written in Java), rather than any reflection of how simple it is to use.

Central to the way that Swing and AWT work together is the notion of components and containers:

Component is the fundamental superclass for all of the Swing library classes. It encapsulates the core functionality of an element of a GUI.

JComponent is a sub class of Component and represents a platform independent GUI element. A JComponent is further sub-classed into, for example, buttons, sliders, frames, panels and all of the rich set of GUI elements and controls. A JComponent is a higher-level GUI elements that does not require a detailed knowledge or interaction with the host Operating System, but instead is concerned with the "look, feel and operation" of the GUI.

A **Container** is a sub class of Component and encapsulates elements of the GUI that require lower level interaction with the host Operating System e.g. to open and close windows. Container services are provided by the AWT. The AWT is responsible for lower level interactions with the host Operating System.

In general, we need not concern ourselves with the operation of AWT container services. They are simply a part of the infrastructure on which Swing rests. Instead we focus on what we want the GUI to be like and how it should operate, and leave the run time issues to the Java Virtual Machine.

To help you understand this difference, here is a partial class hierarchy for the Swing library (package javax.swing):

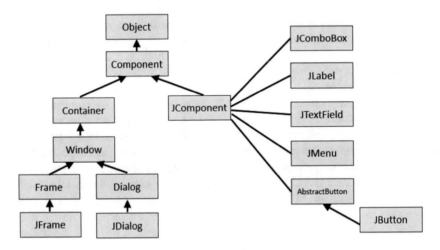

The Object class is, of course, the Java language base object and not part of Swing. We see on the left-hand side aspects of the GUI that require some inter-action with the host Operating System and are thus sub classed from Container, and on the right we see aspects that will interact with those Container derived classes, rather than with the OS in any direct manner and are thus derived from the JComponent class.

8.3   The Taxonomy of a GUI

Before we move on to actually build our very first Swing application, we first need to be clear on some basic terminology that we will use throughout this chapter. A GUI is built from a number of thematic components:

At the highest level, a GUI consists of one or more JFrame. A JFrame is essentially a canvas onto which we assemble all of our other UI elements. A JFrame occupies a window, and that window offers various controls depending on the functionality set out for it.

The JFrame has a section for window controls (the appearance of which is OS dependent) and a contentPane. The contentPane is the surface skin of a JFrame. By default the contentPane is blank.

Onto the contentPane we can place a JPanel. A JPanel is an area where we can place some thematically linked GUI elements e.g. a set of buttons, or buttons and data output displays. A JPanel can also be contain other JPanels.

As an alternative, we can also place GUI elements directly onto the contentPane, and omit the use of a JPanel. This is likely only useful for small GUI designs.

Onto a JPanel we can place a wide range of controls and data display features (taken together "widgets"). These widgets provide us with the fine control requirements of our GUI.

Frames, panels and controls can be made visible and invisible as required to service the needs of the GUI design.

Active controls can have code associated with them to specify what happens when the user interacts with that control. This code is organised in the form of "listeners" that provide for the Controller element of the MVC design pattern. Examples of listeners include responding to button press events and mouse click events. Listeners are required to respond to events asynchronously. We cannot predict when these events will occur, but we must be prepared to respond appropriately to them. So our application becomes driven by GUI events (an "event driven" model) rather than following the predictable model laid out by straight structured and procedural programming.

In general, all useful Swing classes are intended to be sub classed, although we do not need to do so to create a useful GUI.

8.4   A Simple First Swing Application

We are now in a position to build our first Swing application. As is traditional, we shall do with the "Hello World" example. We create a single window program that displays the message and invites the user to press a button (although the button does nothing yet). This program will be built using a thread driven approach (more on this later).

We will take one other important step forwards at this stage and free ourselves from the BlueJ IDE to create a standalone program. This is appropriate here as the point of a GUI is to free us from the constraints imposed by console operation, and create an application that stands on its own merits. Here is the code listing:

```java
import java.awt.*;
import javax.swing.*;

public class HelloWorld implements Runnable
{
    public void run()
    {
        // First create the JFrame window
        JFrame f = new JFrame("Our first Swing application");
        // Determine what happens when the window is closed
        f.setDefaultCloseOperation(WindowConstants.EXIT_ON_CLOSE);
        // Fetch a reference to the JFrame's contentPane
        Container pane = f.getContentPane();
        // Create a JPanel
        JPanel p = new JPanel();
        // Create a button
        JButton b = new JButton("You can press me!");
        // Create a place where we can put some text
        JLabel label1 = new JLabel("Hello World");
        // Add the button and the label to the panel
        p.add(label1);
        p.add(b);
        // Add the panel to the frame
        f.add(p);
        // Pack the frame ready for display
        f.pack();
        // Make the frame visible
        f.setVisible(true);
    }

    public static void main(String[] args)
    {
        // Create an instance of this class
        HelloWorld hw = new HelloWorld();
        // Schedule the application to run
        SwingUtilities.invokeLater(hw);
    }
}
```

From BlueJ, we can just right click the class HelloWorld and select void main(String[] args) and our application will run. All being well, we should see:

We can now see the taxonomy of this GUI application. We see that we create a JFrame, then a JPanel. We add the JButton and the JLabel (a place where text can be displayed) onto the JPanel. We then add the JPanel to the JFrame. The JFrame needs to be "packed" (a process that assigns each element a place on the panel) and then finally make the JFrame visible. The JFrame acquires window controls (it is a sub class of Window) that depend on the OS model (Windows in this case). Clicking the cross on the top right is specified as causing the application to exit. The JButton has been created and can be clicked, but the application has no behaviour to associate with that click event.

In this example, the HelloWorld class has implemented the Runnable interface. Runnable requires implementation of the run() method. Any class that implements this interface will have the run() method invoked automatically when it is instantiated. The application runs on the Event Dispatch Thread using SwingUtilities.invokeLater(). This is considered to be a good way of creating a Swing application as Swing is not "thread safe". A thread is a process on the host machine that executes processes. A host machine will have multiple threads with various applications or processes running on them. A modern OS gives the impression of concurrency by allocating processing time to threads and switching between them. Java programs can be single thread, or multi-threaded. Multi-threaded program design is a complex subject in its own right and beyond the scope of this book. Suffice to say that the job of the Event Dispatching Thread in Java is to update GUI elements promptly as and when required. We can just leave it to its own devices if we choose.

As we have defined a main() method, we are no longer dependent on BlueJ to run our application. To create a fully standalone application, we need to create a Java Archive (JAR) package. A JAR is an archive (set of files organised in a directory) that contains everything needed for the JVM to run our application. The JVM will know how to start the application as it has a main() method. The job of the main() method is to create an instance of a class in the JVM memory and then call appropriate methods to get matters started. We create a JAR file in BlueJ using the "Create JAR file" option under the Project menu. We then identify which class holds the main() method (there can only be one main() method). We then press "continue" and specify where the JAR file is to be stored. The resulting JAR file can then be clicked as any other application. When it is, the JVM identifies the class than holds the main() method and invokes it. We are now free of BlueJ.

We can (and many do) chose to ignore thread management issues; there are alternative ways of organising our first application. We can delegate responsibility for starting up our application to main() and we can build our own sub class from JFrame (a common approach that underlines the fact that Swing components are intended to be sub classed). Here is an alternative version:

```
import java.awt.*;
import javax.swing.*;

public class HelloWorld2 extends JFrame
{
    public HelloWorld2()
    {
      // this now refers to HelloWorld, a sub class
      // of JFrame
      // Determine what happens when the window is closed

      this.setDefaultCloseOperation(WindowConstants.EXIT_ON_CLOSE);
      // Fetch a reference to the JFrame's contentPane
      Container pane = this.getContentPane();
      // Create a JPanel
      JPanel p = new JPanel();
      // Create a button
      JButton b = new JButton("You can press me!");
      // Create a place where we can put some text
      JLabel label1 = new JLabel("Hello World");
      // Add the button and the label to the panel
      p.add(label1);
      p.add(b);
      // Add the panel to the frame
      this.add(p);
      // Pack the frame ready for display
      this.pack();
      // Make the frame visible
      this.setVisible(true);
    }

    public static void main(String[] args)
    {
        // Create an instance of this class
        HelloWorld2 hw2 = new HelloWorld2();
        // Constructor will now be invoked
    }
}
```

In both cases, we could have dispensed with the JPanel and just added the GUI elements directly to the JFrame. But the use of the JPanel is included here for the sake of completeness, and because it represents the more usual way of organising a GUI.

8.5 Event Handling

Our first application has a button that we can press, but nothing happens as yet when we do. We have dealt with the View aspects of the button, but there is no corresponding Controller aspect to go with it. We need to add some code to handle the event of a button press.

Such an event forms just one of the many kinds of events that we might need to manage. Events correspond to user interactions with components:

- Frames are associated with `WindowEvent`.
- Menus are associated with `ActionEvent`.

Java objects can be notified when events occur. These events may occur asynchronously and are detected by "listeners". There are three basic types of listeners:

- **WindowListener**: e.g. detect when the close window icon is clicked, or a window is resized.
- **ActionListener**: e.g. detect when a button is pressed, or the value in a text field is changed.
- **MouseListener**: e.g. detect when a mouse control has been actuated.

At this stage, we are interested in adding an `ActionListener` to deal with a button press event. To do this we create an "anonymous inner class". An inner class is a "class definition within a class definition". It is used where a class is useful in solving some local aspect of a problem, but is not needed more widely than that. An inner class definition has the scope only of the class in which it is defined. An anonymous inner class is simply an inner class that has no need of a specific instance reference name. It is created as a one-off object for which a dedicated class name is not required. It uses a special syntax and it is always reference by its supertype, as it has no sub-type of its own. This anonymous inner class then provides the listener functionality that is then "attached" to our button. We modify our previous example by adding the following method call after we create the `JButton b`:

```
b.addActionListener(
    new ActionListener()
    {
        public void actionPerformed(ActionEvent e)
        {
            label1.setText("Well clicked!");
        }
    }
);
```

The `addActionListener()` method takes one parameter. That parameter is an instance of an `ActionListener` class created by the `new` operator. But the instance has no name and is defined "here and now", hence it is an anonymous instance with type `ActionListener`. `ActionListener` is an abstract class with an obligation to implement one method `actionPerformed()`, so that method definition (yellow box) is contained within the definition of the inner class (green box). In this case, the `actionPeformed()` method calls on a method `setText()` for object `label1` and changes the text on it. The object `label1` is in scope within the definition of the inner class as the inner class is defined within the scope of the enclosing class that declared `label1` in the first place. Note carefully the need to balance the various round brackets and braces.

We can add as many `ActionListener` objects as necessary to provide for all button functionality. Similar listeners are provided for other interactive GUI elements, and we shall see more of them later on. The parameter `e` of type `ActionEvent` for `actionPerformed()` contains information about the event that occurred. We did not need to interrogate `e` in this case, as all we wanted to know was that the button was pressed. When the button is pressed, the `actionPerformed()` method is invoked automatically.

8.6   Centralised and Distributed Event Management

Now that we have a sense of how events are handled, we need a strategy to determine how the potentially large range of events that our GUI could generate should be marshalled. There are two broad options:

- **Have a limited number of centralised event listeners**: when an event happens, we then determine which event it was and act accordingly.
- **Have a distributed set of listeners**: where each GUI element has its own listener and acts independently of all other listeners.

There are no hard and fast rules as to which is the best way to handle events. To understand the difference between these two approaches, we build two example applications with two buttons. First we start with a single centralised event listener:

```java
import java.awt.*;
import java.awt.event.*;
import javax.swing.*;

public class TwoButtonsCentralisedControl implements Runnable
{
    // These elements need to be instance variables so they
    // are accessible throughout the class
    private JButton b1;
    private JButton b2;
    private JLabel label1;

    public void run()
    {
        // First create the JFrame window
        JFrame f = new JFrame("Two buttons");
        // Determine what happens when the window is closed
        f.setDefaultCloseOperation(WindowConstants.EXIT_ON_CLOSE);
        // Fetch a reference to the JFrame's contentPane
        Container pane = f.getContentPane();
        // Create a JPanel
        JPanel p = new JPanel();
        // Create two buttons
        b1 = new JButton("Set to Yes");
        b2 = new JButton("Set to No");
        // Create a place where we can put some text
        label1 = new JLabel("----");
        // Add the button and the label to the panel
        p.add(label1);
        // Create the instance of the centralised listener
        CentralisedListener c = new CentralisedListener();
        // Link the buttons to the listener
        b1.addActionListener(c);
        b2.addActionListener(c);
        p.add(b1);
        p.add(b2);
        // Add the panel to the frame
        f.add(p);
        // Pack the frame ready for display
        f.pack();
        // Make the frame visible
        f.setVisible(true);
    }

    public static void main(String[] args)
    {
        // Create an instance of this class
        TwoButtonsCentralisedControl app =
            new TwoButtonsCentralisedControl();
        // Schedule the application to run
        SwingUtilities.invokeLater(app);
    }

    private class CentralisedListener implements ActionListener
```

```
    {
        // Implement the requirements of the ActionListener
        // interface - provide the actionPerformed() method
        public void actionPerformed(ActionEvent e)
        {
            // Interrogate e ...
            if (e.getSource() == b1)
            {
                label1.setText("Yes");
            }
            else if (e.getSource() == b2)
            {
                label1.setText("No ");
            }
        }
    }
}
```

There are several points to note in this implementation:

- The CentralisedListener is a private inner class. As such its entire class definition is contained within the class definition for TwoButtonsCentralisedControl. The CentralisedListener class cannot be used outside this scope.
- It falls to the enclosing class to instantiate an instance of the private inner class.
- CentralisedListener implements the ActionListener interface and must provide the required actionPerformed() method.
- The variables b1, b2 and label1 have been elevated to instance variables so that they are accessible anywhere within the enclosing class. As the inner class is within the scope of the enclosing class, instance variables are all in scope within the inner class.
- When actionPerformed() is invoked, it needs to determine which of the two buttons was pressed. The object e of type ActionEvent can provide this information using its getSource() method that returns the object reference for the GUI element that caused the event. Once we know which element was the source, we can take appropriate code action.

The alternative approach would be to provide each button with its own listener:

```
import java.awt.*;
import java.awt.event.*;
import javax.swing.*;

public class TwoIndependentButtons implements Runnable
{
    public void run()
    {
        // First create the JFrame window
        JFrame f = new JFrame("Two buttons");
        // Determine what happens when the window is closed
        f.setDefaultCloseOperation(WindowConstants.EXIT_ON_CLOSE);
        // Fetch a reference to the JFrame's contentPane
        Container pane = f.getContentPane();
        // Create a JPanel
        JPanel p = new JPanel();
        // Create two buttons
        JButton b1 = new JButton("Set to Yes");
        JButton b2 = new JButton("Set to No");
        // Create a place where we can put some text
        JLabel label1 = new JLabel("----");
        // Add the button and the label to the panel
        p.add(label1);
        // Link independent listeners for the buttons
        b1.addActionListener(new ActionListener()
            {
                public void actionPerformed(ActionEvent e)
                {
                    label1.setText("Yes");
                }
            }
        );
        b2.addActionListener(new ActionListener()
            {
                public void actionPerformed(ActionEvent e)
                {
                    label1.setText("No ");
                }
            }
        );
        p.add(b1);
        p.add(b2);
        // Add the panel to the frame
        f.add(p);
        // Pack the frame ready for display
        f.pack();
        // Make the frame visible
        f.setVisible(true);
    }

    public static void main(String[] args)
    {
        // Create an instance of this class
        TwoIndependentButtons app =
```

```
            new TwoIndependentButtons();
        // Schedule the application to run
        SwingUtilities.invokeLater(app);
    }
}
```

In this example, each button operates independently of the other and has its own anonymous inner class to provide a response to its own click event.

Both programs work just fine. In general, most Swing coders will tend to opt for the distributed model. The centralised model works, but tends not to scale to larger applications very well, resulting in very large sections of centralised code.

8.7 Applying the MVC Design Pattern

By now, the broad sense of how Swing is designed should be becoming clear. But thus far we have made some simple GUI applications, but they haven't had much of a useful purpose other than to demonstrate core Swing concepts. Now we consider integrating a GUI with a useful underlying application.

The underlying application is our MVC model. It should not concern itself with any aspect of the GUI. In turn, the GUI will provide the View and Controller elements. The View elements include `JLabel`, the `JFrame` and the `JPanel` and so on. The Controller elements are provided by event handlers. It is worth observing that Swing does have a tendency in practical implementations to blur the separation of the View and Controller aspects of the MVC design pattern, as the code for the event handlers is very much integrated into the GUI code base. It is certainly possible to completely the separate the two, and the centralised event management example gives insight as to how this might be achieved. But in practice the combined View and Controller arrangement works just fine. The critical separation is between the GUI and the Model.

To help us develop our ides, we shall build a small MVC style application with the following specification:

- There shall be two buttons, one labelled "increase" and the other "decrease".
- A number is displayed on the GUI, starting with an initial value of 0.
- Pressing either button shall increase or decrease the displayed number by 1.
- The displayed number has a minimum value of 0 and a maximum value of 10.
- If the user tries to increase or decrease the displayed number outside of these bounds a dialog box shall appear to advise them of the limit.

Not the most interesting specification, but it will serve as a useful example. First, we focus on the underlying application logic and create a class `NumberApp`:

```java
public class NumberApp
{
    private int value;
    public NumberApp()
    {
        value = 0;
    }

    public String getValueAsString()
    {
        return value + ""; // Turns the int into a String
    }

    /**
     * Increases value by 1
     * @return true if value is < 10, false otherwise
     */
    public boolean incValue()
    {
        if (value < 10)
        {
            value++;
            return true;
        }
        else
        {
            return false;
        }
    }
    /**
     * Decreases value by 1
     * @return true is value is > 0, false otherwise
     */
    public boolean decValue()
    {
        if (value > 0)
        {
            value--;
            return true;
        }
        else
        {
            return false;
        }
    }

    public void resetCount()
    {
        value = 0;
    }
}
```

The `NumberApp` class provides all of the code necessary to make the application work, but nothing in respect of a GUI. It does provide a set of `public` methods that the GUI will need to work with it. The model part is capable of executing without an GUI, and that is significant as it also means that it is suited to automated testing using a `JUnit` test class:

```
@Test
public void test()
{
    NumberApp n = new NumberApp();
    // value should be zero initially ...
    assertEquals(n.getValueAsString(),"0");
    // try to decrease by 1, should stay at 0 ...
    n.decValue();
    assertEquals(n.getValueAsString(),"0");
    // Increase to 3 ...
    n.incValue();
    n.incValue();
    n.incValue();
    assertEquals(n.getValueAsString(),"3");
    // reset to 0 ...
    n.resetCount();
    assertEquals(n.getValueAsString(),"0");
    // Increase to 10;
    for (int i=0; i<10; i++)
    {
        n.incValue();
    }
    assertEquals(n.getValueAsString(),"10");
    // Try to inc again, should stay at 10
    n.incValue();
    assertEquals(n.getValueAsString(),"10");
}
```

Automated testing of the GUI element is harder to realise. Typically, the GUI elements would need to be tested either under control of an application scripting language, or a documentation led process of system testing.

Now we can build a GUI to provide the View and Controller elements. The GUI will need to:

- Create an instance of the `NumberApp` class.
- Create all of the GUI elements.
- Link the GUI elements to the public methods in `NumberApp`.

Here is our GUI code listing:

```
import java.awt.*;
import java.awt.event.*;
import javax.swing.*;

public class NumberAppGUI implements Runnable
{
    // An instance of Number app is required
    private NumberApp app;

    public NumberAppGUI()
    {
        // Create an instance of NumberApp
        app = new NumberApp();
    }

    public void run()
    {
        // First create the JFrame window
        JFrame f = new JFrame("Number app");
        // Determine what happens when the window is closed
        f.setDefaultCloseOperation(WindowConstants.EXIT_ON_CLOSE);
        // Fetch a reference to the JFrame's contentPane
        Container pane = f.getContentPane();
        // Create a JPanel
        JPanel p = new JPanel();
        // Create two buttons
        JButton up = new JButton("Up");
        JButton down = new JButton("Down");
        // Create a place where we can put some text
        JLabel label1 = new JLabel(app.getValueAsString());
        // Add the button and the label to the panel
        p.add(label1);
        // Link independent listeners for the buttons
        up.addActionListener(new ActionListener()
            {
                public void actionPerformed(ActionEvent e)
                {
                    if (app.incValue() == true)
                    {
                        label1.setText(app.getValueAsString());
                    }
                    else
                    {
                        showWarning(f);
                    }
                }
            }
        );
        down.addActionListener(new ActionListener()
            {
                public void actionPerformed(ActionEvent e)
                {
                    if (app.decValue() == true)
                    {
```

```
                              label1.setText(app.getValueAsString());
                    }
                    else
                    {
                        showWarning(f);
                    }
                }
            }
        );
        p.add(up);
        p.add(down);
        //Set the contentPane size
        pane.setSize(220,100);
        p.setPreferredSize(new Dimension(240,120));
        // Add the panel to the frame
        f.add(p);
        // Pack the frame ready for display
        f.pack();
        // Make the frame visible
        f.setVisible(true);
    }

    public void showWarning(JFrame f)
    {
        JDialog d;
        d = new JDialog(f, "Alert");
        d.setSize(100,100);
        JLabel x = new JLabel("Range 0 to 10!");
        d.setLocation(250,200);
        d.add(x);
        d.setVisible(true);
    }

    public static void main(String[] args)
    {
        // Create an instance of this class
        NumberAppGUI gui = new NumberAppGUI();
        // Schedule the application to run
        SwingUtilities.invokeLater(gui);
    }
}
```

Some points to note:

- The GUI is responsible for creating the instance of the underlying application. It does this conveniently using its constructor. The constructor is invoked as soon as the static main() method creates the instance of the NumberAppGUI class.
- The code adds an example of a JDialog used to provide a user alert. The dialog box could have been further equipped with a button to close it.
- The code uses setSize(), setPreferredSize() and setLocation() methods to exercise a more fine-grained control over where things appear on the screen.

- The GUI communicates with the underlying application via the `app` object reference.

We could redesign the GUI at any stage without having to change anything of the `NumberApp` class. Thus we have achieved a strong separation of how an application looks to how it functions. This is the separation of concerns that we aspire to in good GUI driven application development.

8.8 Adding Menus, Text Fields, Text Areas and Images

Now that we are familiar with some Swing basics, we can start to investigate the large range of components that it offers. There are substantive texts devoted to the components and much available online. In this section we explore a selection of useful components.

Menus are commonplace in modern GUI design. They form a part of a `JFrame` (actually part of the `Window` super class). and are used to provide over-arching functionality such as opening files, printing and quitting the application. We can easily add some menu options to our existing programs.

JMenuBar: the menu bar element of a `JFrame`.

JMenu: a component to hold a set of menu options for the `JFrame`. The options will generally form some thematic set of related operations (but they do not have to).

JMenuItem: a selection option that appears on a `JMenu`.

We shall add two menu options under a thematic heading "Options". The two options will be:

- To display a `JDialog` box with information about the application ("about" option).
- To quit the application ("quit" option).

We add some new methods to our application:

```
public void makeMenuBar(JFrame f)
{
    JMenuBar m = new JMenuBar();
    // set the menu bar for the frame f
    f.setJMenuBar(m);
    // Create the "Options" menu
    JMenu optionsMenu = new JMenu("Options");
    // Now add some items to the menu
    JMenuItem aboutItem = new JMenuItem("About");
    JMenuItem quitItem = new JMenuItem("Quit");
    // Now we add some listeners for the menu items
    aboutItem.addActionListener((event) -> showAbout(f));
    quitItem.addActionListener((event) -> System.exit(0));
    // Add the items to the menu
    optionsMenu.add(aboutItem);
    optionsMenu.add(quitItem);
    // Finally, add the menu to the menu bar
    m.add(optionsMenu);
}

public void showAbout(JFrame f)
{
    JOptionPane.showMessageDialog
        (f,"Created by Kingsley Sage \nEnjoy!");
}
```

We then call makeMenuBar() at some point in the build of our GUI prior to packing and making the frame visible. Note the method requires the object reference to the parent JFrame as a parameter. There are some other notable points:

- Each of the JMenuItem objects is equipped with an ActionListener to specify what they will do when selected. In this case a syntactic shorthand has been adopted based on an innovation since Java 8—the introduction of lambda expressions into the language. A full ActionListener can also be provided and there are situations where that is appropriate.
- The method System.exit() causes the JVM to terminate the application. The parameters associated with the method call provides a status code to the host OS on the situation that lead to the shutdown. A parameter of 0 indicates a normal controlled exit.
- The JOptionPane static utility class can be used to easily make a variety of commonplace warning and information popups.
- The menu bar appears at the top left of our application.

Although somewhat advanced for this book, a lambda expression is matched against the parameter type of the method (addActionListener() in this case). If the expression matches the parameter type, then the lambda expression is turned into a function that implements the same interface. Lambda expressions can only be used where the type they are matched against is a single method interface (such as

ActionListener). This is an example of the functional programming paradigm. In our case, it's a compact and convenient syntactic form to set up our event listeners.

JTextField is a component that allows for the editing of a single line of text and is thus useful for user textual input. In contrast, JTextArea allows for the display and editing of multi-line text. Here is an example of both in practice:

```java
import java.awt.*;
import java.awt.event.*;
import javax.swing.*;

public class TextExamples implements Runnable
{
    public void run()
    {
        // First create the JFrame window
        JFrame f = new JFrame("Some text examples");
        // Determine what happens when the window is closed
        f.setDefaultCloseOperation(WindowConstants.EXIT_ON_CLOSE);
        // Fetch a reference to the JFrame's contentPane
        Container pane = f.getContentPane();
        // Create a JPanel
        JPanel p = new JPanel();
        // Create a JTextField with 20 columns
        JTextField t1 = new JTextField(20);
        t1.addActionListener(
          (event) -> textAction1(f,t1.getText()));
        // Create a JTextArea with 20 rows and 20 columns
        JTextArea t2 = new JTextArea(5,20);
        JScrollPane scrollPane = new JScrollPane(t2);
        scrollPane.setVerticalScrollBarPolicy
              (JScrollPane.VERTICAL_SCROLLBAR_ALWAYS);
        t2.setEditable(true); // true by default
        t2.setText("Some text \non several lines");
        // Add to the panel
        p.add(t1);
        // Note we add the scrollPane, not t2 to the panel
        p.add(scrollPane);
        // Add the panel to the frame
        f.add(p);
        // Pack the frame ready for display
        f.pack();
        // Make the frame visible
        f.setVisible(true);
    }

    public void textAction1(JFrame f, String text)
    {
        JOptionPane.showMessageDialog(f,text);
    }
    public static void main(String[] args)
    {
        // Create an instance of this class
        TextExamples t = new TextExamples();
        // Schedule the application to run
        SwingUtilities.invokeLater(t);
    }
}
```

Some points worthy of note:

- The JTextField has an event associated with it when the user presses the enter key.
- We have once again used the lambda expression to provide the ActionListener for the JTextField.
- The JTextArea has been placed inside a JScrollPane component that provides for user configurable scroll bars. Note that it is the JScrollPane object we ended up adding to the panel, not the JTextArea object.

This should now start giving the confidence to investigate the online documentation to find out more about these useful classes. Our application looks like this:

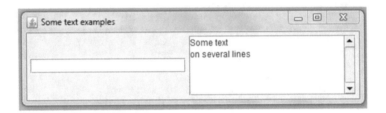

Of course, no discussion of GUIs would be complete without adding some images. The Java ImageIcon class (curiously not beginning with a J) is very suitable for general background image and general icon work. We can add ImageIcon objects to labels, buttons and a whole host of other components. The images themselves need to be stored somewhere rooted within the project folder where you Java JAR file or BlueJ project lives. This directory information is dependent on the host machine, so we need to use a method to get a Uniform Resource Locator (URL) for it. Here are just two examples of adding an ImageIcon to a JLabel and a JButton:

```java
import java.awt.*;
import java.awt.event.*;
import javax.swing.*;

public class UsingImages implements Runnable
{
    public void run()
    {
        // First create the JFrame window
        JFrame f = new JFrame("Some text examples");
        // Determine what happens when the window is closed
        f.setDefaultCloseOperation(WindowConstants.EXIT_ON_CLOSE);
        // Fetch a reference to the JFrame's contentPane
        Container pane = f.getContentPane();
        // Create a JPanel
        JPanel p = new JPanel();
        // Create an image for the button
        String path1 = "/resources/image1.png";
        java.net.URL imgURL1 =
            UsingImages.class.getResource(path1);
        ImageIcon icon1 = new ImageIcon(imgURL1);
        // Create the button
        JButton b1 = new JButton("",icon1);
        // Add an ActionListener for completeness
        b1.addActionListener((event) -> showMessage(f));
        // Add to the panel
        p.add(b1);

        // Create an image for the JLabel
        String path2 = "/resources/image2.png";
        java.net.URL imgURL2 =
            UsingImages.class.getResource(path2);
        ImageIcon icon2 = new ImageIcon(imgURL2);
        JLabel k1 = new JLabel("",icon2,JLabel.CENTER);
        p.add(k1);

        // Add the panel to the frame
        f.add(p);
        // Pack the frame ready for display
        f.pack();
        // Make the frame visible
        f.setVisible(true);
    }
    public void showMessage(JFrame f)
    {
        JOptionPane.showMessageDialog(f,"It's a nice button");
    }
    public static void main(String[] args)
    {
        // Create an instance of this class
        UsingImages i = new UsingImages();
        // Schedule the application to run
        SwingUtilities.invokeLater(i);
    }
}
```

All being well, we get a button with an image on it, and a still image next to it:

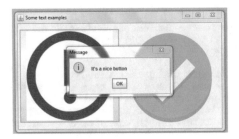

Some points worthy of note:

- The images are stored in a folder called resources located in the project root folder. We used a static method from our own class to recover the URL path to that folder. This makes our application portable.
- Resizing images on the fly is not trivial. Our button icon is rather large! It is best to prepare button icons at the size you intend them to be used.

At this point, we notice that although we are doing well in creating many basic components of our GUI and getting them to do something useful, we have little in the way of fine grained control over where everything appears on the screen estate. The spatial organisation of the GUI components needs to be managed by yet another component—the layout managers.

8.9 Layout Managers

As the name suggests, the job of a layout manager is to determine how all the GUI components are set out in a Container (such as a JFrame). The layout manager determines the minimum, maximum and preferred sizes for the container as it appears on the screen and then lays out the container's children i.e. the components added to the container. If a child component has its own layout manager then it is in turn laid out by that manager. You are not required to use a layout manager (and our examples thus far have not), but the default for containers if the FlowLayout.

There is a range of different layout managers that are suited to different basic GUI designs.

FlowLayout: The default layout. Components appear from in a flow direction (typically left to right) depending on the order they were added to the container and will move when the window is resized.

BoxLayout: components are organised in a single row or column and are not resized when the container is resized.

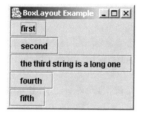 

BorderLayout: components can be organised into five areas.

GridLayout: components are equally sized and are arranged in rows and columns.

GridLayout Example	_ □ ×
first	second
the third string is a long one	fourth
fifth	

GridBagLayout: a powerful layout whereby components are organised using a grid, but components can span more than one cell.

GridBagLayout	_ □ ×
One	Two	Three
Four		
		Five
Six	Seven	

You can also use:

- **CardLayout**: Different components can appear at different times.
- **GroupLayout**: Permits separate organisation of horizontal and vertical components.
- **SpringLayout**: Defines relationships between the edges of components.

To use a layout manager, you pass an instance of the manager to the constructor of the container. You can also set after construction using a setLayout() method. Once a layout manager has been associated with the container, then you generally (depending on the layout manager) pass additional parameters to the add () method when adding components to the container to specify the constraints or other parameters associated with adding the component to the container under the auspices of the layout manager.

For example, we can create a simple 3 × 3 grid of JLabels under control of a GridLayout manager. Note that the grid co-ordinate system has the origin (x = 0, y = 0) at the top left of the container, with increasing y values going down the container. Here, the add() method needs no new parameters as the grid is filled in a pre-determined order:

```java
import java.awt.*;
import javax.swing.*;
import javax.swing.border.Border;

public class GridLayoutExample implements Runnable
{
    public void run()
    {
        // First create the JFrame window
        JFrame f = new JFrame("GridLayoutExample");
        // Determine what happens when the window is closed
        f.setDefaultCloseOperation(WindowConstants.EXIT_ON_CLOSE);
        // Fetch a reference to the JFrame's contentPane
        Container pane = f.getContentPane();
        // Create a JPanel organised using GridLayout
        // with a horizontal and vertical gap of 10
        JPanel p = new JPanel(new GridLayout(3,3,10,10));
        // Add a 3 x 3 grid of JLabels
        for (int y=0; y<3; y++)
        {
            for (int x=0; x<3; x++)
            {
                // Show position as (x,y)
                JLabel j = new JLabel("(" + x +"," + y +")",
                        SwingConstants.CENTER););
                // Add a border to the label
                Border b =
                    BorderFactory.createLineBorder(Color.BLACK);
                j.setBorder(b);
                // Add to the panel
                p.add(j);
            }
        }
        // Add the panel to the frame
        f.add(p);
        // Pack the frame ready for display
        f.pack();
        // Make the frame visible
        f.setVisible(true);
    }

    public static void main(String[] args)
    {
        // Create an instance of this class
        GridLayoutExample g = new GridLayoutExample();
        // Schedule the application to run
        SwingUtilities.invokeLater(g);
    }
}
```

Resulting in:

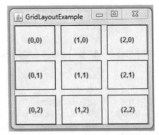

As another example, we can create a simple GUI using `BorderLayout` with four buttons at the edge of the screen and a label occupying the centre region:

```java
import java.awt.*;
import javax.swing.*;
import javax.swing.border.Border;

public class BorderLayoutExample implements Runnable
{
    public void run()
    {
        // First create the JFrame window
        JFrame f = new JFrame("BorderLayoutExample");
        // Determine what happens when the window is closed
        f.setDefaultCloseOperation(WindowConstants.EXIT_ON_CLOSE);
        // Fetch a reference to the JFrame's contentPane
        Container pane = f.getContentPane();
        // Create a JPanel organised using BorderLayout
        JPanel p = new JPanel(new BorderLayout());
        // Add a label to the centre panel
        JLabel l1 = new JLabel("The Centre",
                    SwingConstants.CENTER);
        l1.setPreferredSize(new Dimension(100,100));
        p.add(l1,BorderLayout.CENTER);
        // Add some buttons
        JButton b1 = new JButton("North");
        JButton b2 = new JButton("South");
        JButton b3 = new JButton("East");
        JButton b4 = new JButton("West");
        p.add(b1,BorderLayout.NORTH);
        p.add(b2,BorderLayout.SOUTH);
        p.add(b3,BorderLayout.EAST);
        p.add(b4,BorderLayout.WEST);
        // Add the panel to the frame
        f.add(p);
        // Pack the frame ready for display
        f.pack();
        // Make the frame visible
        f.setVisible(true);
    }

    public static void main(String[] args)
    {
        // Create an instance of this class
        BorderLayoutExample b = new BorderLayoutExample();
        // Schedule the application to run
        SwingUtilities.invokeLater(b);
    }
}
```

This time, add() has an additional parameter to specify which zone we wish to add the component to. The code produces this output:

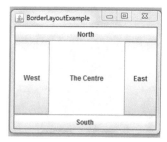

It takes some experimentation to work out which is the best layout manager for any specific GUI design. There is no single correct approach, and with time you will develop you own workflow preferences and strategies. Swing is an extensive library and it will take time to master it.

It is worth noting that Swing is not the only option for building a GUI in Java. JavaFX is an alternative platform for building both desktop and rich Internet applications for a wide range of devices. JavaFX was developed originally by Sun Microsystems and is now owned by Oracle and it is likely that JavaFX will eventually replace Swing as the standard approach for Java GUI development, but the two will likely co-exist for many years to come, and as with all new libraries and toolkits, it can be difficult to predict what the dominant thinking in GUI design will be in decades to come.

Example Applications

9

In this final chapter, we look at two examples of Java applications to consolidate the knowledge we have gained in this book. We consider a practical workflow for designing and developing an OO program to help us understand some of the broader software engineering issues associated with good coding.

The two examples are very different and have been chosen to illustrate different aspects of Java. The first example is the Good Life Foods project. It is an exercise in getting class design right, but does not consider GUI design. The second example builds on the Guessing Game example we first saw in Chap. 2 and focusses on improving the underlying code and incorporating a Swing GUI. Both projects can be found in the electronic copies of the code that accompanies this book. You should take the time to look at these code projects and use them to affirm and develop your understanding of the key concepts discussed throughout this book.

9.1   Software Engineering Process Models

In software engineering, a process model is simply a set of rules, or a strategy, for the means that are used to develop a solution a solution to a problem. Simply booting up your machine and writing code with no pre-planning is unlikely to deliver a well-crafted and robust solution, if indeed it delivers a solution at all. Software engineering is a broad subject in its own right, but we can highlight two popular process models that are widely used to solve practical problems:

- **Waterfall**: a classical approach:

  - start with a set of user requirements (in the client's own terms), leading to
  - development of formal requirements, leading to

© Springer Nature Switzerland AG 2019
K. Sage, *Concise Guide to Object-Oriented Programming*,
Undergraduate Topics in Computer Science,
https://doi.org/10.1007/978-3-030-13304-7_9

- design process, followed by
- implementation (coding), then
- testing, and finally
- delivery.

- **Agile**: a more modern approach:

  - Requires a close working partnership with the client.
  - An iterative process based around short "sprints" that result in the delivery of a series of incremental prototypes for evaluation.
  - Prior to each sprint, a set of "user stories" is selected that describe some element of the user's requirement.
  - A sprint, under the leadership of a "scrum master" works intensively to deliver that capability.
  - Iterative development continues until the product meets the user's requirements.

The analysis of the relative merits of these two approaches continues to be a popular debate in the software development community. But either way, they still involve making good choices for code, and both still require us to make use of good OO design and coding skills. Poor code is still poor code whatever the underlying process model.

9.2   The Good Life Foods Project

For this project, we will start with a statement of the user's requirements. User requirements are simply a free body of text that describes what our end user or customer would like to achieve in their own words. It should not contain any descriptions of how the solution should be coded, or any other significant technical details—that is down to the development team. Our role will be to consider the user requirements, and to determine an appropriate set of OO classes that we can use to produce a working solution. The user requirements for this project are as follows:

"Good Life Foods sells and delivers fruit, vegetables and healthy cakes via on-line ordering. Customers can order any quantity of products to form an order. Fruit and vegetables are ordered either by integer quantity (e.g. 3 bananas) or by weight (e.g. 3 kg of potatoes). Heathy cakes are ordered as individual items and can be produced with customised messages (such as "Happy Birthday").

In order to be economic, an order must have a total value of more than £10. For orders that are between £10 and £30, Good Life Foods will charge for delivery at £5. For orders over £30 the delivery is free. You may assume that the data necessary to generate the orders can be provided by a search operation. You do not need to define that search operation. Whenever a customer uses the site, they must register so that they can provide delivery address details. They can then search the site for the items they want, and generate an order with all the items added to their order.

When the user has finished choosing items, they place their order. The content of their order is then displayed on the screen, along with the cost of delivery and the total cost. Customers can also delete items from their order before it is finally placed. Good Life Foods staff need to be able to track their orders so they need to be able to recover the order details by a unique reference number assigned to each order so that any problems in the order can be dealt with later."

We now consider what OO classes are needed to solve this problem. We remind ourselves of a set of general principles that we should embrace. Consider it your "coding manifesto":

- **Cohesion**: each class should represent one useful entity and do it well.
- **Coupling**: we should aim to minimise, as far as practicable, interactions between classes.
- **Encapsulation**: data and methods should remain `private` unless they need to be `public`. A class API should consist of only those things that are necessary for the class to do its job.
- **Responsibility driven design**: It an entity should be responsible for performing some behaviour, then the corresponding class should implement it.
- **Consider factorising sets of class where relevant**: so that classes with a common ancestry or basic purpose share a common super class. This promotes code re-use and avoids code duplication.
- **Defensive coding**: don't provide obvious and easily preventable causes of failure.
- **Extensibility**: code in a manner that permits reasonable future enhancements and development.
- **Documentation**: provide meaningful comments and use Javadocs documentation conventions.
- **Coding style**: use appropriate variable names, and follow basic coding conventions.
- **Test classes**: consider adding unit test classes to automate the process of testing that your classes are operating correctly.

Looking at the user requirements, we identify some candidate classes:

Candidate class	Description
Customer	A user of the shop
Fruit	A fruit item that a customer can order
Vegetable	A vegetable item that a customer can order
HealthyCake	A cake item that a customer can order
Order	A set of items that the customer can order
GoodLifeFoods	The shop as a whole, that has customers and items available for order

As part of this process we may find that the user requirements:

- use more than one word to describe the same entity (synonyms) e.g. "customer" and "user" refer to the same entity.
- are incomplete.
- are vague.
- refer to entities at different level of abstraction e.g. "all of the items" and "fruit", "vegetables" and so. on

But nonetheless, the set of classes we have are a reflection of the requirements. We further refine these using our OO design principles. Note the word "item" keeps on reappearing in the candidate list above—that is a clear clue to the existence of a super class. We therefore refine our thinking and produce a proposed set of actual class for development. We also select appropriate collection types:

- An Order is clearly an unordered list of items, so the ArrayList is a good choice. A Customer "owns" the Order.
- The Good Life team need to be able to recover orders by a unique reference, so a HashMap is a good choice for storing the collection of all customer orders as the order can be recovered in constant time using a String (the uniqueReference) as the key.

We can then start to assign attributes and methods into our proposed set of Java classes. It is often simpler to start with attributes first, since the method signatures will require prior knowledge of the attribute types. We also note that there is an obvious OO super class for any item that Good Life Foods sells. Out attribute set looks like this:

Class	Attributes

Customer	`String lastname;`
	`String firstname;`
	`String address;`
	`Order myOrder;`

Item	`String name;` `double unitCost`
Fruit extends Item	`int quantity;`
Vegetable extends Item	`double weight;`
HealthyCake extends Item	`String msg;`

Order	`String uniqueReference;`
	`ArrayList < Item > allItems;`
	`double costOfItems;`
	`double deliveryCharge;`

GoodLifeFoods	`HashMap < String,Customer > allOrders;`

We double check this list of attributes covers all of the needs of the original user requirements and it appears to be suitable. This process may require several iterations to get right. There is no single solution, just ones that make sense, and everything else.

Now we can determine what methods are needed. For clarity, we can ignore accessor and mutator methods as it is likely that all classes will need them to some extent. We might need to consider whether multiple constructor methods are required. As long as we engage in sufficient design to make the path to our development clear, we will have done enough. We also need to consider whether any `static` (factory/utility) methods are required. Here is a list of possible key `public` methods:

Class	Key methods

Customer	`void addItemToOrder(Item i);`
	`void deleteItemFromOrder(int i);`
	`void displayDetailsOfOrder();`
	`void summariseOrder();`

Item	`abstract double calculateCost();` `abstract void describeItem();`
Fruit extends Item	`double calculateCost();` `void describeItem();`
Vegetable extends Item	`double calculateCost();` `void describeItem();`
HealthyCake extends Item	`double calculateCost();` `void describeItem();`

Order	`void summarise();`
	`double calculateTotalCost();`
	`int getNumberOfItems();`

(continued)

(continued)

Class	Key methods
GoodLifeFoods	registerCustomer(String firstname, String lastname, String address); void placeOrderForCustomer(Customer c); Customer recoverOrder(String uniqueReference); static String genUniqueReference();

Note that GoodLifeFoods is responsible for generating unique reference String data. Generating such data does not particularly require an instance of the class to be instantiated, and it is likely that other classes will need to generate unique references e.g. when an order is generated. As a means of testing our ideas, we can further create a test class. The project includes a test class CustomerTest that gives a sense of how this design is intended to operate:

```java
@Test
/** Create a customer, add some items to their order.
 */
public void placeAnOrder()
{
    Customer c = new Customer("Smith","John","1 The Avenue");

    c.addItemToOrder(new Fruit("Apples",0.20,5));
    c.addItemToOrder(new Vegetable("potatoes",1.0, 2.0));
    c.addItemToOrder(new HealthyCake("Chocolate Cake",
                10.00, "Happy Birthday"));

    // Delete the potatoes for now ...
    c.deleteItemFromOrder(1);
    assertEquals(c.getOrder().getNumberOfItems(),2);

    // Calculate the costs and delivery charges
    // 5 apples and the cake should be £11.00
    // with a delivery charge of £5.00.
    // Costs are compared to the nearest penny.
    double cost = c.calculateTotalCost();
    assertEquals(cost,16.00,0.01);

    // Summarise the order ...
    c.summariseOrder();

}
```

The final BlueJ class diagram (including the test class) looks like this:

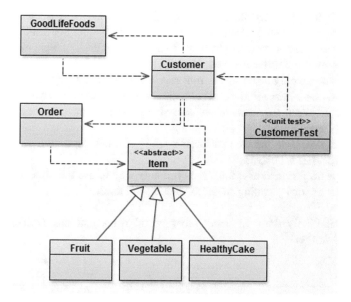

We note that:

- GoodLifeFoods does not have an association with Order. An Order is an attribute of a Customer in this design.
- The association from Customer to GoodLifeFoods is on account of the factory method that generates uniqueReference field.
- An Order is a collection of Item.
- The assertEquals() method in CustomerTest needs to compare two double values. Such a comparison needs to be performed to a specified degree of accuracy. In this case that tolerance was set to £ 0.01 = 1 penny.

This is just one possible design. You should examine the full code listing to make sense of what each of these methods actually does.

There are many ways that the existing Good Life Foods project could be improved. If you want to develop the project further, here are some suggestions for improvements:

- There are no validity checks on the supplied parameters for any of the classes. E.g. we can create an Item with a negative cost, or set the address of a Customer to a blank String.
- The Item objects are being created "on the fly" within the Customer class. So a Customer could devise any Fruit, Vegetable or HealthyCake they imagined to purchase. In reality, GoodLifeFoods sell from a stock list, and

that should be represented in the `GoodLifeFoods` class, and the `Customer` should then select from this list.

- There is no guarantee that the `uniqueReference` field is unique, as it is produced by a random number generator. A truly unique number could be generated using a more sophisticated strategy possibly manipulating the time and day that the order was placed.
- An `Item` can only be removed from an Order using knowledge of its position in the `myOrder ArrayList`. This exposes more of the underlying design that we would wish. Removal of an Item should be by name, or some other user friendly means.
- There is no check that the `Customer` who generates the `Order` has registered with `GoodLIfeFoods`.
- There is no practical user interface. The only way to use the project is either by test classes, or by calling methods directly in BlueJ.

You will likely think of many other useful ways that this project could be developed further.

9.3 The Guessing Game Project

For this project, we revisit the simple game project we first used in Chap. 2, but we make further enhancements to it, and build a suitable GUI to go with it. As before, we shall start with a statement of our user requirements:

> "The guessing game is a simple game that requires us to guess a randomly generated number between 1 and 100 (inclusive). Users may then make up to 10 guesses to find the right answer. If the guess is too high or too low, an appropriate message should be generated. The game ends when the user has either guessed the answer correctly, or has had 10 turns.
>
> The user should be able to end the game early by retiring, when the answer will be shown. If a user guesses a number that they have previously entered, then a message should be displayed and that turn will not count to the total of current turns used. The game should be GUI driven".

This game does not really require a multiple class solution. There is only really one underlying entity and that is the game itself. However, we do want a GUI, and the MVC design pattern requires us to separate the underlying application logic from the GUI. By way of an analysis, we come up with a list of the attributes and methods that the underlying `GuessingGame` class will require:

Attribute	Description
`int answer;`	The answer generated by the game
`int numTurns;`	The current number of turns the user has made.
`int[] allGuesses;`	An array of `int` containing all the guesses the user had made
`private int maxTurns;`	The maximum number of turns the user may make

Method	Description
`public int getTurns()`	Accessor for the current number of `turns`
`public int getAnswer()`	Accessor for the correct `answer`
`public int getMaxTurns()`	Accessor for `maxTurns`
`public int analyseGuess (int guess)`	Analyse the current `guess`. Return –2 if the `guess` has been tried before, –1 if the `guess` is too low, +1 if the `guess` is too high, and 0 if the `guess` is correct
`private boolean triedThatAlready(int guess)`	Returns `true` if the guess has been tried before, `false` otherwise
`public void resetGame()`	Resets all game attributes to suitable default values

We also draw up a list of the GUI features that will be required:

- Three menu options:

  - To find "about" information.
  - To retire from the game. The answer should be displayed.
  - To quit.

- A `JTextField` where we can enter our guess. Pressing enter will validate our guess.
- A `JLabel` where the current number of guesses is displayed.
- A `JLabel` where messages for "Too high" and "Too low" can be displayed.

We decide to use a simple `GridLayout` to manager the GUI. In the complete code project you will see how these features have been achieved. By way of good practice, a test class has also been included for the underlying `GuessingGame` as it is able to function independently of its GUI. We have enough information already in our design to specify how the test class should operate:

```
@Test
public void test1()
{
    int someGuess;
    GuessingGame game = new GuessingGame();
    int x = game.getAnswer();
    someGuess = x - 1;
    // someGuess is too low ...
    assertEquals(game.analyseGuess(someGuess),-1);
    assertEquals(game.getTurns(),1);
    someGuess = x + 1;
    // someGuess is too high ...
    assertEquals(game.analyseGuess(someGuess),1);
    assertEquals(game.getTurns(),2);
    // Try that guess again. Should be marked
    // as a repeat guess.
    assertEquals(game.analyseGuess(someGuess),-2);
    // Try the right answer ...
    someGuess = x;
    assertEquals(game.analyseGuess(someGuess),0);
    // Check maxTurns ...
    assertEquals(game.getMaxTurns(),10);
}
```

By way of completeness, here is the BlueJ class diagram:

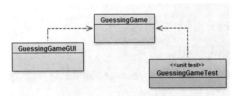

We start the game either by invoking main() from BlueJ, or we can assemble a JAR file for standalone operation. If we do, we see the form of the GUI:

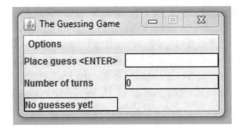

9.4 Final Thoughts

The two examples shown in this chapter should provide insight into the broad OO design process and stimulate you into developing them further to develop your understanding of writing good Java programs.

The Java landscape is large, with ever growing libraries for you to investigate and use in your own applications. Part of the skill of being a good coder is to have the intuition that "if a class seems to solve a useful problem often" then there probably is a class in a library somewhere that does what you need. Once you locate it, the key to getting the benefit from it is the ability to use the API documentation properly.

Programming is, in many respects, part science, part common sense, and part creative. This last point reflects the fact that there are inevitably a large number of ways that any problem can be solved, each with their own relative merits. The more you code, the more you think about the way that you code. Discuss coding with others—even hardened professionals find new ways of solving problems through dialogue with other. There is always something new to be learned, and a new way of looking at an old problem.

Above all, learn to think ahead about what you do. The Object Oriented paradigm is very powerful, and Java delivers on it, but it is worth reflecting in a modern world dominated by technology and software systems that the most powerful tool in creating programs and applications is our imagination, a pen and paper, an analytical mind and a good cup of tea.

Index

A
Abstract class, 90
Abstract method, 90
Abstract Window Toolkit (AWT), 151
Access-modifier, 30
Accessor, 53, 54
Action, 26
ActionEvent, 157
ActionListener, 157
Ada Lovelace, 5
addActionListener(), 168
@After, 111
Agile, 180
Alan Turing, 3
Algorithms, 5, 130
Alteration, 22
Alternation, 20
Alternative orderings, 131
Analytical engine, 3
Android, 8
Android Runtime, 8
Annotations, 65
Anonymous inner class, 157
Application Programming Interface (API), 47,
    63
ArithmeticException, 122
Array index, 125
ArrayIndexOutOfBoundsException,
    125
ArrayList, 67, 123
Array of arrays, 129
Arrays, 124
Arrays.sort(), 130
Artificial Intelligence, 3
ASCII code, 2
assertEquals(), 112
Assignment operator, 23
@author, 66
Autocode, 5

Automated testing, 164

B
Base class, 76
@Before, 111
Behaviour, 14, 41
Bletchley Park, 4
BlueJ, 9
BlueJ inspector, 49
Bombe, 4
boolean, 17
BorderLayout, 173
BoxLayout, 173
Braces, 14
break, 24
Breakpoints, 106
Buckets, 138
BufferedReader, 119
byte, 17, 72
Byte code, 7

C
C, 5
C++, 7
Call, 106
Call sequence, 106
Call stack, 20
CardLayout, 174
case, 24
Central panel, 12
char, 17
charAt(), 62
Charles Babbage, 2, 3
Checked exceptions, 118
Child class, 76
.class, 11
Class, 7, 13, 39, 43
Class attribute, 18
Class diagram, 49

© Springer Nature Switzerland AG 2019
K. Sage, *Concise Guide to Object-Oriented Programming*,
Undergraduate Topics in Computer Science,
https://doi.org/10.1007/978-3-030-13304-7

Class level polymorphism, 77
Class library, 57
Class variable, 95
COBOL, 5
Code libraries, 57
Code re-use, 59
Coding defensively, 101
Coding syntax errors, 100
Cohesion, 63, 181
Collections, 131
Collections.sort(), 133
Collection type, 124
Colossus, 4
Commenting, 65
Comments, 14
Comparable, 132
Comparator, 131, 132
compareTo(), 61, 133
compareToIgnoreCase(), 61
Compile, 5, 13
Component, 151
Component level testing, 108
Concatenation operator, 19
Constants, 95
Constructor method, 45
Container, 152
contentPane, 153
Controller, 150
Coupling, 181

D
Dalvik, 8
Debugger, 106
Declaring an object, 50
default, 25, 94
Defensive coding, 181
Design errors, 101
Design patterns, 63, 149
Difference Engine, 3
Digital control, 1
Documentation, 181
Double, 17, 72
do .. while loop, 26, 28
Duplicate key, 140
Dynamic type, 88

E
else ... if, 23
Encapsulation, 40, 63, 181
ENIAC, 4
Enigma, 3
Entity, 40
Environmental errors, 101

Equality operator, 23
Event Dispatch Thread, 155
Event driven, 153
Exception, 117
extends, 78
Extensibility, 181

F
Ferranti Mk 1, 4
Field of a class, 18
finally, 118
Fit for purpose, 114
Fixed length arrays, 123
Flavors, 7
float, 17
FlowLayout, 172, 173
for loop, 26
For each loop, 70
Formal-parameters, 30
FORTRAN, 5
Fully qualified name, 58
Function, 15, 29

G
Garbage collection, 47
Graphical User Interfaces (GUIs), 147
GridBagLayout, 174
GridLayout, 173
GroupLayout, 174

H
Has-a, 56
hashCode(), 137
Hash function, 137
HashMap, 138
HashSet, 141
Hash table, 137
hasNext(), 143
Hello World, 11
Hierarchical structures, 75
Highly cohesive, 39
Human Computer Interaction (HCI), 147

I
if, 22
ImageIcon, 170
Immutable, 60
import, 34
import directive, 58
Infinite loop, 28
Inheritance, 80
Inherited, 79
Initialising an object, 50

Initial-state, 26
Inspector, 44, 104
Instance, 16
Instance variable, 18
int, 17
Integer, 72
Integrated Development Environment (IDE), 8
Interface, 92
Interpreted, 5
IOException, 118
Is-a, 56
Is-a relationship, 77
isEmpty(), 114
Iteration, 20, 25, 103
Iterator, 143
iterator(), 143

J
Jacquard weaving loom, 1
Jacques de Vaucanson, 2
Jagged arrays, 129
Jakarta EE, 8
Jakarta framework, 57
.java, 11
Java, 7
Java Archive (JAR), 155
Java class, 16
Java Development Kit (JDK), 8
Javadocs, 64
JavaFX, 177
Java object, 16
Java operators, 23
Java Virtual Machine (JVM), 7
JButton, 155
JComponent, 151
JDialog, 167
JFrame, 153
JMenu, 167
JMenuBar, 167
JMenuItem, 167
JOptionPane, 168
Joseph-Marie Jacquard, 1
JPanel, 153
JRE, 8
JTextArea, 169
JTextField, 169
JUnit, 164

K
Key, 138
Key-value pair, 138

L
Layout manager, 172

length, 125, 129
Linear probing, 137
List, 141
Listeners, 153
Loading factor, 139
Logical operators, 24
Logic errors, 100
long, 17, 72
Loop, 25

M
main(), 96, 155
main() method, 97
Manchester Mk 1, 4
Map, 141
Map.Entry, 144
Mathematical operators, 18
Member function, 43
Menu bar, 12, 167
Menu options for, 167
Method, 29
Method polymorphism, 87
Method variable, 19
Minimally coupled, 40
Model, 150
Model View Controller (MVC), 150
MouseListener, 157
Multi line comments, 14
Multiple inheritance, 82
Mutator, 53, 54
Mutator method, 102

N
Natural order, 130
next(), 143
null, 127
NullPointerException, 117

O
Oak, 7
Object, 7, 43, 80
Object reference, 50
OO coding, 37
OO design, 37, 76
Oracle Corporation, 8
Organisational unit, 39
Override, 83
@Override, 83

P
Package, 59
@param, 66
Parent class, 76, 77
Polymorphism, 77

Primitive data, 17
private, 30, 83
Private vs. public, 40
Procedural programming, 14, 19
protected, 83
public, 15, 30, 83
Public method, 14
Punched paper cards, 1

R
Random, 32
Random number, 32
Repetition, 20, 25
Reset the JVM, 28
Responsibility driven design, 181
@return, 66
Return statement, 30
Return-type, 30
Reverse order, 131
Rules of scope, 18
run(), 155
Run time errors, 101
RunTimeException, 118

S
Scala, 63
Scanner, 32
Selection, 20, 22
Self-referential operator, 51
Sequence, 20
Set, 141
setLayout(), 174
setLocation(), 166
setPreferredSize(), 166
setSize(), 166
setText(), 158
setUp(), 111
short, 17, 72
Short Code, 5
Simula, 6
Single line comments, 14
Singleton class, 46
Smalltalk-80, 6
Sorting, 130
SpringLayout, 174
State, 41
Static class, 46
Static type, 88
Static variable, 95
String, 45, 59
Strongly typed language, 17
Structured programming, 19
Structured test schedule, 116

Structured walkthrough, 104
Sub class, 76
Sun Microsystems, 7
Super and sub class, 56
Super class, 76, 81
Super keyword, 81
Swing, 148
switch, 22, 24
System, 15
System class, 15, 46
System.exit(), 168
System level testing, 108, 116
System.out.println(), 15
System testing, 164

T
Task decomposition, 20
teardown(), 111
@Test, 112
Test-condition, 26
Test Driven Development (TTD), 114
this, 45, 51, 81
Throwable, 118
Throws an exception, 117
toLowerCase(), 46
toString(), 80
toUpperCase(), 46
Tree diagrams, 75
trim(), 114
try and catch, 117
Turing machine, 3
Two dimensional arrays, 127

U
Uncaught exception error, 117
Unit level testing, 108
Unit test class, 108
User errors, 101
User requirements, 180
Utility class, 95

V
@version, 66
View, 150
void, 15
Void method, 29

W
Waterfall, 179
while loop, 26
Widgets, 153
Window, 155
WindowEvent, 157

`WindowListener`, 157
Workbench, 12
Wrapper class, 72
Write Once, Run Anywhere (WORA), 7

Z
Zero indexed, 62
Zero referenced, 125